Really Interesting Stuff You Don't Need to Know

1,500 Fascinating Facts

David Fickes

Introduction

By nature, I tend to collect trivia without trying. Until relatively recently, I had never sought out trivia; however, after creating a holiday trivia presentation for a community party and then showing it at one of our fitness studio's spinning classes, I found myself creating weekly trivia. The cycling clients enjoyed the diversion of answering questions while they exercised, so I continued.

I have tried to ensure that the information is as accurate as possible, and to retain its accuracy, I have also tried to avoid facts that can quickly change with time. This book is intended for people who prefer to read interesting facts rather than quiz themselves with questions and answers. Since the information isn't in a question and answer format, it also allows different types of facts that aren't as well suited for a quiz format.

There are 1,500 fascinating facts covering a wide range of topics including animals, arts, history, literature, miscellaneous, movies, science and nature, sports, television, U.S. geography, U.S. presidents, and world geography. This is book 1 of my *Really Interesting Stuff* series; I hope you enjoy it, and if you do, look for other books in the series.

Contents

Facts 1-300

1) Based on oxygen usage, the jellyfish is the most efficient swimmer of any animal. Jellyfish use 48% less oxygen than any other known animal; they never stop moving.

2) India has the most public holidays of any country with 21; Colombia and Philippines are second with 18.

3) O.J. Simpson was the original choice to play the title role in *The Terminator* before Arnold Schwarzenegger got the part. Director James Cameron thought he was too likable among other things.

4) Damascus, Syria is the oldest continuously inhabited city in the world; it has been inhabited for at least 11,000 years.

5) Abraham Lincoln was the first Republican president.

6) One million dollars in $100 bills weighs about 20.4 pounds.

7) Due to inflation, Argentina has changed the value of its currency by a factor of 10 trillion since 1970.

8) You would get vitamin A poisoning and could die if you ate a polar bear's liver. Polar bears have 50-60 times the normal human levels of vitamin A in their liver, and it is about three times the tolerable level that a human can intake.

9) Moscow, Russia has the world's busiest McDonald's restaurant.

10) New Zealand was the first country to allow women to vote in 1893.

11) The chameleon has the longest tongue relative to its size of any animal.

12) Cats can't taste sweet. They don't have taste receptors for sweet; this applies to all cats domestic and wild.

13) Peter Finch in 1976 for *Network* and Heath Ledger in 2008 for *The Dark Knight* are the only two people to win posthumous acting Oscars.

14) Besides his moose strength, Bullwinkle Moose's great talent was that he could remember everything he ever ate.

15) The expression "red–letter day" derives from a custom of using red ink on calendars to indicate religious holidays.

16) In *Gilligan's Island*, the *S.S. Minnow* was named after Newton Minow who was head of the Federal Communications Commission (FCC). Sherwood Schwartz, the show's creator, did not care for Minow who had called television "America's vast wasteland", so he named the soon to be shipwrecked ship after him.

17) The word muscle comes from the Latin musculus which means little mouse because a flexed muscle was thought to resemble a mouse.

18) Academy Awards are called Oscars because Margaret Herrick, Academy librarian and future executive director, thought the statue looked like her uncle Oscar.

19) Walnuts, almonds, pecans, and cashews aren't technically nuts; they are drupes which also include peaches, plums and cherries. Drupes are a type of fruit where an outer fleshy part surrounds a shell or pit with a seed inside. For some drupes, you eat the fleshy part, and for some, you eat the seed inside.

20) All seven dwarfs except Dopey have a beard.

21) For a few seconds, a horse can generate about 15 hp; for sustained output over hours, a horse can generate about one hp.

22) George Washington, Thomas Jefferson, Andrew Jackson, Martin Van Buren, and Dwight Eisenhower were all redheads.

23) With 17 million units sold, the Commodore 64, introduced in 1982 with a 1 MHz processor and 64K of memory, is the biggest selling personal computer model of all time.

24) Gold is the most malleable naturally occurring metal.

25) Mount Chimborazo, Ecuador is closer to the Moon than any other place on Earth. It is 20,548 feet elevation but very close to the equator, so the bulge in the Earth makes it 1.5 miles closer to the Moon than Mount Everest.

26) The jawbone is the hardest bone in the human body.

27) When a woodpecker's beak hits a tree, it experiences 1,000 times the force of gravity.

28) Ronald Reagan was the first U.S. president to have been divorced.

29) Glenn Miller received the first ever music gold disc for "Chattanooga Choo Choo" in 1942.

30) The most common team name for U.S. college football teams is Eagles.

31) Oklahoma City and Indianapolis are the only two state capitals that include the name of the state.

32) *The Flintstones* in 1960 was the first animated prime time series on U.S. television.

33) Wi-Fi doesn't stand for anything. It doesn't mean wireless fidelity or anything else; it is just a branding name picked by a company hired for the purpose.

34) Humans have about 5 million olfactory receptors; dogs have about 220 million.

35) Mark Twain was the first novelist to present a typed manuscript to their publisher.

36) If the Moon didn't exist, a day on Earth would be 6-8 hours long.

37) Sheep grazed in New York's Central Park until 1934; they were moved during the Great Depression for fear they would be eaten.

38) Edith Head has won more Oscars than any other woman; she won eight for costume design.

39) At 10 years old, Tatum O'Neal is the youngest competitive Oscar winner ever for *Paper Moon* (1973).

40) Only Michael Jackson, Madonna, U2, and Weird Al Yankovic have had top 40 hits in each of the last four decades (1980s, 1990s, 2000s, 2010s).

41) Coffee originated in Ethiopia in the 11th century.

42) Abraham Lincoln's first choice to lead the Union army was Robert E. Lee.

43) Macy's was the first U.S. department store in 1858.

44) Pure water isn't a good conductor of electricity; the impurities in water make it a good conductor.

45) The Bluetooth wireless technology is named after King Harald "Bluetooth" Gormsson who ruled Denmark in the 10th century.

46) Deion Sanders is the only person to ever play in the Super Bowl and World Series.

47) Elizabeth Taylor was the first film star to earn $1 million for a single film for *Cleopatra* in 1963.

48) The Ruppell's Griffon vulture is the highest-flying bird species ever recorded. They have been spotted at 37,000 feet and have special hemoglobin which makes their oxygen intake more effective.

49) Although he was 73 years old at the time, Frank Sinatra had to be first offered the role of John McClane in *Die Hard.* The movie is based on the book *Nothing Lasts Forever* which was a sequel to *The Detective* which had been made into a movie in 1968 starring Sinatra, so contractually, he had to be offered the role first.

50) In the movie *Lifeboat*, Alfred Hitchcock couldn't make his usual in person cameo appearance because the film was set in a lifeboat, so he appears as a before and after picture in a newspaper weight loss ad.

51) The national animal of Scotland is the unicorn.

52) In the Grimm's fairy tale, the *Pied Piper of Hamelin* is described as pied because he wears a two-colored coat; pied is thought to come from magpie birds which are black and white.

53) While floating in lunar orbit, astronaut Al Worden became the most isolated human ever; he was 2,235 miles from the nearest human while in the *Apollo 15* command module.

54) With an estimated 500 million copies sold, *Don Quixote* is the best-selling fiction book of all time; *A Tale of Two Cities* is second at about 200 million copies.

55) Richard Nixon once carried three pounds of marijuana for Louis Armstrong. In 1958, Vice President Richard Nixon ran in to Louis Armstrong at Idlewild Airport in New York. Since he didn't have to go through customs, Nixon offered to carry Armstrong's luggage. Without knowing it, Nixon carried three pounds of marijuana for Armstrong.

56) Catfish have more taste buds than any other animal. They have over 100,000 taste buds both in their mouth and all over their body; humans have about 10,000.

57) *It Happened One Night* (1934), *One Flew Over the Cuckoo's Nest* (1975), and *The Silence of the Lambs* (1991) are the only three films to win all five major Academy Awards (best picture, director, actor, actress, screenplay).

58) Mark Twain is generally credited with first saying "When in doubt, tell the truth."

59) President George W. Bush was a head cheerleader in high school.

60) Pikes Peak in Colorado was the inspiration for the song "America the Beautiful."

61) The hippopotamus produces its own sunscreen. It produces a mucus like secretion that keeps them cool and acts as a powerful sunscreen.

62) The last public execution in the U.S. was in 1936 in Kentucky.

63) Alaska receives the least sunshine of any state.

64) One in 10,000 people have perfect pitch, the ability to identify a musical note just by hearing it with no reference note.

65) Influenza killed an estimated 43,000 U.S. servicemen mobilized for WWI; it accounted for about half of all U.S. military deaths in Europe.

66) Kansas is the geographic center of the 48 contiguous states.

67) Elvis Presley memorized every line from his all-time favorite movie *Patton*.

68) There are 13 witches in a coven.

69) In 1956, *The Wizard of Oz* was the first feature film broadcast on U.S. television.

70) Texas and Oklahoma share the longest border of any two states at 700 miles.

71) Rod Stewart played to 4.2 million people on Copacabana Beach in Rio de Janeiro, Brazil on New Year's Eve 1994 in the largest free rock concert ever held.

72) Florence Nightingale carried a pet owl with her in her pocket.

73) Saturn is the only planet in our solar system less dense than water.

74) The cheerleader effect is a bias that causes people to think that individuals are more attractive when they are in a group likely due to the averaging out of unattractive idiosyncrasies.

75) The longest table tennis rally (single point) at an international competition lasted for 2 hours and 12 minutes with an estimated 12,000 hits. It was the opening point of a 1936 world championship match; game time limits were later put in place.

76) The adult human body has about 100,000 miles of blood vessels.

77) Cleopatra was born 2,500 years after the Great Pyramid of Giza was built; she was closer to our current time than she was to the pyramids.

78) The television series *Lost in Space* was set in 1997.

79) Ronald Reagan is the oldest person to win a U.S. presidential election; he was 73 at time of his re-election.

80) California is the only state that is at least partially north of the southernmost part of Canada and at least partially south of the northernmost point of Mexico.

81) Many nursing homes in Germany have fake bus stops to collect residents and stop dementia residents from leaving.

82) Kellogg Corn Flakes were invented in a sanitarium in 1894.

83) Musicians as a group have the life expectancy of Zimbabwe, the lowest of any country in the world.

84) *The Godfather Part II* and *The Lord of the Rings: The Return of the King* are the only two sequels to win Best Picture Oscars.

85) Crab in *Two Gentlemen of Verona* is the only named dog in any Shakespeare play.

86) Captain Crunch's full name is Captain Horatio Magellan Crunch.

87) Without your pinky finger, you would lose 50% of your hand strength.

88) Seven basketball players have won NCAA, Olympic, and NBA championships - Clyde Lovellette, Bill Russell, K.C. Jones, Jerry Lucas, Quinn Buckner, Michael Jordan, and Magic Johnson.

89) Boxing originated the term southpaw. Left-handed fighters were said to use a southpaw stance; no one is quite sure why but hitting someone with a left came to be known as a southpaw punch.

90) The first enclosed climate-controlled mall in the U.S. was opened in 1956 in Edina, Minnesota.

91) In the sport of curling, pebbling the rink ice is done to create some friction for the stone to curl. Ice preparers sprinkle the ice with tiny water droplets which freeze on the surface of the ice to create a pebbled texture.

92) Husband and wife Emil and Dana Zatopek both won gold medals at the 1952 Helsinki Summer Olympics. Emil won the 5,000 meters,

10,000 meters, and marathon despite never running a marathon before; Dana won the javelin.

93) Extirpation is local extinction; the species is extinct locally but still exists elsewhere.

94) Benjamin Franklin's image is engraved on the Pulitzer Prize gold medals.

95) The probability of a human living to 110 years or more is about 1 in 7 million.

96) Tokyo, Japan has more millionaires than any other city.

97) The classic film *It's a Wonderful Life* originated from a Christmas card. Philip Van Doren Stern had written a short story, *The Greatest Gift*, and had unsuccessfully tried to get it published. He sent it out as a 21-page Christmas card to his closest friends; a producer at RKO Pictures got hold of it and purchased the movie rights.

98) Benjamin Franklin earned an honorary induction into the International Swimming Hall of Fame. He had a lifelong love of swimming and was an ardent proponent of it and invented some swim fins.

99) Adjusted for inflation, *Gone with the Wind* is the all-time highest grossing movie in the U.S.; it is followed by *Star Wars*, *The Sound of Music*, *E.T. the Extra-Terrestrial*, and *Titanic*.

100) The bald eagle's name comes from the old English word piebald which means white headed.

101) Chinese checkers originated in Germany in 1892.

102) Due to air resistance, the fastest a human body can fall is about 120 mph; this is known as terminal velocity.

103) In Sanskrit, the word Himalayas means house of snow.

104) The United States has the most domestic cats of any country in the world; China has the second most.

105) At 5.5 million square miles, the Antarctic Polar Desert is the largest desert in the world.

106) Google is the world's most visited website.

107) Kobe Bryant is the only person to win an Olympic gold medal and an Oscar; he won Olympic basketball gold medals in 2008 and 2012 and Best Animated Short Film for *Dear Basketball* in 2018.

108) The band Led Zeppelin got their name because another musician said their band would go down like a lead balloon.

109) Armadillos are good swimmers, but they also walk underwater to cross bodies of water. They can hold their breath for 6-8 minutes.

110) The most sweat glands on the human body are on the bottom of the feet.

111) U.S. television allows alcohol to be advertised if no alcohol is consumed in the commercial; it isn't a law or FCC regulation just a broadcasting standard.

112) Pablo Picasso's work is stolen more than any other painter.

113) Queen Elizabeth II is the longest reigning British monarch; she surpassed her great great grandmother Victoria's reign in 2015.

114) Nevada has the highest percentage of federal land of any state with 81%; Utah is second at 66%.

115) Nine presidents never attended college – Washington, Jackson, Van Buren, Taylor, Fillmore, Lincoln, Andrew Johnson, Cleveland, Truman

116) After Apollo 11 landed on the moon and before anyone set foot on the moon, Buzz Aldrin took communion; NASA did not want it broadcast or made public.

117) The Incas first domesticated guinea pigs and used them for food, sacrifices, and household pets.

118) Louis Braille developed the Braille system for the blind at the age of 15 and published the first book about it at age 20.

119) Joseph Priestley who later discovered oxygen invented carbonated soda water.

120) Horses can't breathe through their mouths. A soft palate blocks off the pharynx from the mouth except when swallowing.

121) Dudley Do-Right's horse was named Horse.

122) The tallest mountain in the known universe is 69,459-foot Olympus Mons on Mars.

123) William Shakespeare has more films based on his work than any other author.

124) The Huston and Coppola families have three generations of Oscar winners; Walter, John, and Anjelica Huston and Carmine, Francis Ford, and Sofia Coppola have all won Oscars.

125) The first arrest for marijuana possession and selling in the United States occurred in 1937 in Colorado.

126) The average person produces 25,000 quarts of saliva in their lifetime.

127) Antarctica is the only place on earth that doesn't have a time zone.

128) Three presidents have won Grammys for best spoken word album – Clinton, Carter, Obama.

129) Wrigley's gum was the first product to have a barcode.

130) Five surnames – Adams, Harrison, Johnson, Roosevelt, Bush – have been shared by more than one president. Only Andrew and Lyndon Johnson weren't related.

131) Cats are crepuscular animals which means that they are active primarily during twilight hours – just after dawn and before dusk.

132) In 1942, a German V2 rocket was the first man made object in space; 62 miles above sea level qualifies as space.

133) Balloons were originally made from animal bladders.

134) Canada is the only host country not to win a gold medal at its own summer Olympics at the 1976 Montreal games.

135) Elvis Presley's natural hair color was sandy blonde.

136) George Washington was the only president to never live in Washington, D.C.

137) Based on land area, Yakutat, Alaska is the largest city in the U.S.; at 9,459 square miles, it is larger than the state of New Hampshire.

138) The caribou or reindeer are the only animal species where females have antlers.

139) The top 1% of bands and solo artists earn 77% of all recorded music revenue.

140) Five countries have effectively 100% literacy rates – Andorra, Finland, Liechtenstein, Luxembourg, and Norway.

141) In ancient Ireland, sucking a king's nipple was a sign of submission.

142) Laurence Olivier for *Hamlet* (1948) and Roberto Benigni for *Life Is Beautiful* (1997) are the only two people to direct themselves to a best actor or best actress Oscar.

143) The Tom Hanks movie *The Terminal* was inspired by a man who lived at the departure lounge of Charles de Gaulle International Airport for 18 years.

144) The novel *Les Misérables* was given to all officers in the Confederate army during the U.S. Civil War. Robert E. Lee believed the book symbolized their cause.

145) In math, a lemniscate shape means infinity; lemniscate is the word for a shape with two loops meeting at a central point.

146) Iceland's phone book is alphabetized by first name; everyone is referenced by their first name. They don't have surnames in the traditional sense; the surname is their father's first name suffixed with either son or daughter.

147) *The Lord of the Rings: The Return of the King* (2003) is the only fantasy film to win the Best Picture Oscar.

148) Ribbon worms will eat themselves if they can't find food. They can eat a substantial portion of their body and still survive.

149) In Denmark, a svangerskabsforebyggendemiddel is a condom. This is the official term; there is a shorter more common term, gummimand.

150) The dot over the letter "i" is called a tittle.

151) During WWII, India had the largest volunteer army in world history with 2.5 million soldiers.

152) Silver currently makes up 92.5% of an Olympic gold medal.

153) Pumice is the only rock that floats in water.

154) Butterflies taste with their feet.

155) Adjusted for inflation, *Snow White and the Seven Dwarfs* (1937) is the highest grossing animated movie of all time in the U.S.

156) Under the original terms of the U.S. Constitution, the president didn't choose his own vice president; the candidate with the second most electoral votes was vice president.

157) The Mpemba Effect is the phenomenon where hot water may freeze faster than cold.

158) The Decalogue is more commonly known as the Ten Commandments.

159) A lethal dose of chocolate for a human would be about 22 pounds. Theobromine is a powerful stimulant in chocolate and can cause death in high enough doses.

160) Horse racing's Triple Crown has only been won once in consecutive years; Seattle Slew and Affirmed won in 1977 and 1978.

161) A group of rattlesnakes is called a rhumba.

162) Eighty percent of the world's population eats insects as part of their regular diet.

163) Estivation is the summer equivalent to hibernation. During estivation, animals slow their activity for the hot, dry summer months.

164) It takes an income of $32,400 to be in the top 1% of the world.

165) From 1912 to 1948, the modern Olympics included music, painting, poetry, literature, and architecture.

166) Graca Machel is the only first lady in the world to be first lady of two countries. She is the widow of both South Africa President Nelson Mandela and Mozambique President Samora Machel.

167) King Nebuchadnezzar who built the Hanging Gardens of Babylon is the best-known historical sufferer of the psychological disorder boanthropy where the sufferer believes they are a cow or ox. In the Book of Daniel, Nebuchadnezzar "was driven from men and did eat grass as oxen."

168) Nauru is the only country in the world without an official capital. It is the third smallest country in the world in the central Pacific and has less than 10,000 people.

169) The Greenland shark has the longest known lifespan of all vertebrate (with a backbone) animal species. They can live up to 400 years.

170) The "no animals were harmed" statement on movies only applies when film is recording.

171) Heroin was introduced by Bayer in 1898 and marketed as a non-addicting alternative to morphine and a treatment for cough inducing illnesses like bronchitis. The AMA approved it for general use in 1906 and recommended it as a morphine replacement; soon, there were 200,000 heroin addicts in New York City alone.

172) Australia has the world's longest fence; it is the dingo fence completed in 1885 and is 3,488 miles long.

173) In Roman times, men held their testicles as a sign of truthfulness when bearing witness in public.

174) David is the most frequently mentioned name in the bible; Jesus is second.

175) There are five debt free countries in the world – Macau, British Virgin Islands, Brunei, Liechtenstein, and Palau.

176) Lake Zaysan in eastern Kazakhstan is the oldest lake in the world at about 65 million years.

177) The opossum has more teeth (50) than any other land mammal.

178) The prop used for Dr. McCoy's medical scanner in the original *Star Trek* television series was a salt shaker.

179) Wabash, Indiana was the world's first electrically lighted city in 1880.

180) The Stanley Cup is the oldest championship in North American professional sports; it started in 1893.

181) There are more English words beginning with the letter s than any other letter.

182) The first chocolate treat was hot chocolate during the Aztec civilization.

183) The camellia sinensis evergreen shrub produces tea.

184) The tardigrade, a water dwelling, 8-legged micro animal about one-half mm long, can survive temperatures as low as –458 degrees and as high as 300 degrees Fahrenheit for several minutes, 1000 atmospheres of pressure, radiation hundreds of times higher than the lethal dose for humans, the vacuum of space, and can live for 30 years without food or water. They were discovered in 1773 and are found everywhere from mountain tops to deep sea and tropical to Antarctic.

185) Great Britain is the only country that is exempt from the international rule that a country's name must appear on its postage stamps. They were the first country with postage stamps and had no name on them and were exempted when the rule was made.

186) In September 1989, Deion Sanders hit an MLB home run and scored an NFL touchdown in the same week. He is the only person ever to do it.

187) Silver is the best conductor of electricity of any metal; it is slightly more conductive than copper but much more expensive.

188) Churches in Malta have two clocks to confuse the devil; one clock has the right time, and one has the wrong time.

189) *The Simpsons* is the longest running U.S. scripted prime time show ever; it started in 1989.

190) At age 70, Benjamin Franklin was the oldest person to sign the Declaration of Independence; the average signer was 44 years old.

191) On average, sharks kill 12 people per year worldwide.

192) Mexico is the foreign country visited most by Americans.

193) Four-time Oscar winning actress Katharine Hepburn was the Connecticut state golf champion at age 16.

194) Leonardo da Vinci could write with both his left and right hand simultaneously.

195) Badminton is the fastest racquet sport; the shuttlecock can travel over 200 mph.

196) The hippopotamus is responsible for the most human deaths of any of the large African animals.

197) Alaska was purchased from Russia in 1867 for two cents per acre.

198) Canada is the only country in the world where more than 50% of its adults have college degrees.

199) There are 108 stitches on a regulation baseball.

200) The ancient Greeks used olive oil instead of soap to clean themselves; they rubbed it into their skin and then scraped it off along with dirt and dead skin.

201) Berlin still hasn't gotten back to its pre-WWII population.

202) The greatest distance any human has ever been from Earth is 248,655 miles aboard *Apollo 13*.

203) Eighty-eight percent of the world's population lives in the Northern Hemisphere. About half of the world's population lives north of 27 degrees north latitude.

204) More than 90% of all jury trials in the world occur in the United States.

205) Four presidential candidates have won the popular vote but lost the election – Andrew Jackson against John Quincy Adams, Samuel Tilden against Rutherford B. Hayes, Al Gore against George W. Bush, and Hilary Clinton against Donald Trump.

206) Budweiser was the first nationally distributed beer in the U.S.

207) A starfish is the only creature that can turn its stomach inside out.

208) The dots on dice are called pips.

209) The band Jethro Tull was named after the inventor of the seed drill.

210) With four miles to go in the 2004 Athens men's marathon, Vanderlei de Lima of Brazil who was leading by almost 30 seconds was tackled to the ground by a spectator. Officials arrived and pulled the spectator off, and de Lima continued the race, but he was subsequently caught and passed and ended up winning the bronze medal. He filed a protest which was not upheld.

211) Michelangelo was struck in the face by a rival with a mallet and disfigured for life.

212) In total darkness, most people naturally adjust to a 48-hour cycle instead of 24 hours. They have 36 hours of activity followed by 12 hours of sleep; the reasons are unclear.

213) A kangaroo can hop at 40 mph.

214) Joseph Biden was the first Roman Catholic U.S. vice president.

215) At age 63, Barbara Bush was the oldest first lady at time of inauguration.

216) Venus and Uranus are the only two planets in our solar system that rotate clockwise.

217) The pronghorn antelope is the second fastest land animal behind the cheetah. Pronghorns can achieve speeds of 55 mph.

218) Acmegenesis is better known as an orgasm.

219) Cate Blanchett is the first person to win an acting Oscar portraying a real acting Oscar winner; she won the Best Supporting Actress Oscar for portraying Katharine Hepburn in *The Aviator* (2004).

220) Adjusted for inflation, *The Exorcist* is the only horror film to gross $1 billion in the U.S.

221) Sunglasses were invented in China to hide the eyes of judges.

222) The original move *TRON* in 1982 was not considered for a visual effects Oscar because they felt the filmmakers had cheated by using computers.

223) *It's a Wonderful Life* (1946), *Miracle on 34th Street* (1947), and *The Bishop's Wife* (1947) are the only three Christmas movies ever nominated for the Best Picture Oscar.

224) The Atlantic Ocean is the saltiest ocean.

225) Since 1863, Norway has published all personal tax returns for everyone to see; you can see total income and total taxes for anyone. In 2014, they added the restriction that the person whose information is being requested will be notified who is looking which has resulted in far fewer inquiries.

226) By area, Manitoulin island in Lake Huron, Ontario Canada is the largest freshwater island in the world; it is over 1,000 square miles.

227) South America has more Roman Catholics than any other continent.

228) The word ukulele literally means jumping flea likely after the movements of the player's fingers.

229) The ostrich is the fastest two-legged animal; it can reach speeds over 40 mph.

230) The feeding of the 5,000 is the only miracle mentioned in all four gospels of the Bible.

231) Charles Darwin is credited as being the first person to put wheels on an office chair around 1840.

232) The Catholic church made Galileo recant his theory that the Earth revolves around the Sun; it took them 359 years to declare Galileo was right in 1992.

233) Actor Paul Newman finished runner-up in the Le Mans 24-hour auto race.

234) A priest was the first person to propose the big bang origin of the universe; Georges Lemaitre's work preceded Edwin Hubble.

235) Kevin Smith's comedy movie *Clerks* is loosely based on Dante's *The Divine Comedy* from the 14th century. The main protagonist, Dante Hicks, gets his name from this, and there are nine breaks in the film to represent the nine rings of hell.

236) It would take 1.2 million mosquitoes each sucking once to drain the average human of all their blood.

237) *The Howdy Doody Show* (1947-1960) was the first nationally televised children's show in the U.S.

238) Stephenie Meyer, the author of the *Twilight* books, chose the real town of Forks, Washington as the setting for the books because the city has the most rainfall in the contiguous 48 states and is small, out of the way, and surrounded by forest. She had never been there.

239) The Earth is the densest planet in our solar system.

240) Polish businessman, beautician, entrepreneur and inventor Max Factor coined the word makeup in 1920.

241) Of the Earth's total water, 96.5% is in the oceans.

242) Michael Crichton is the only author to have his works simultaneously number one in television, film, and books with *ER* (television), *Jurassic Park* (film), and *Disclosure* (book).

243) The four states of matter observable in everyday life are solid, liquid, gas, and plasma.

244) *Gone with the Wind* and *All the King's Men* are the only two Pulitzer Prize winning novels made into Best Picture Oscar winners.

245) The Sun orbits around the center of the Milky Way Galaxy at a speed of 536,865 mph.

246) New York City is the most linguistically diverse (highest number of languages spoken) city in the world with 800 languages spoken.

247) Captain James Cook was the first man to set foot on all the continents other than Antarctica.

248) *The Ladies' Mercury* in 1693 was the world's first periodical designed and published for women.

249) Kiribati is the only country that falls in all four hemispheres; it is an island nation in the central Pacific.

250) Alfred Hitchcock appeared in more than 30 Alfred Hitchcock films.

251) During a 10-day period in 2001, Argentina had five presidents; it was during an economic crash combined with defaulting on foreign debt.

252) The original name for Los Angeles was El Pueblo de Nuestra Señora la Reina de los Ángeles del Río Porciúncula.

253) The Indonesian word for water is air.

254) Ice hockey originated in the United Kingdom. There are references to similar games being played on ice in England, Scotland, and Ireland going back 200 years before the first documented game in Canada.

255) Ojos Del Salado on the Chile & Argentina border is the highest active volcano in the world at 22,595 feet.

256) *Dumbo* (1941) was the first Disney animated feature set in present day at the time of its release.

257) Australia's first police force was composed entirely of criminals; the best-behaved convicts were selected.

258) Manny Pacquiao won world titles in the largest number of boxing weight divisions; he held titles in eight divisions - flyweight, super bantamweight, featherweight, super featherweight, lightweight, light welterweight, welterweight, super welterweight.

259) Bing Crosby was first offered the role of television's Lt. Colombo.

260) Planck time is the smallest named time interval; it is the length of time required for light to travel a Planck length or 5.39×10^{-44} seconds.

261) Africa has more French speakers than any other continent; it has 120 million French speakers.

262) A sapiosexual is sexually attracted to intelligence in others.

263) The highest percentage of Americans are sleeping at 3:00 am, about 95.1%.

264) A human can live unprotected in space for about 30 seconds provided they don't hold their breath. You would be unconscious in about 15 seconds; if you hold your breath, your lungs explode.

265) *Gone with the Wind* was the first full color film to win the Best Picture Oscar.

266) Elvis Presley's only three Grammy awards were for gospel music. Much of his main work was before the Grammys existed.

267) Good King Wenceslas was king of Bohemia, the current Czech Republic.

268) Peppermint was the first Lifesaver flavor.

269) A polyandric women has more than one husband.

270) Humans need 16 to 20 images per second to perceive something as a moving picture rather than a flickering image; dogs need 70 images per second. Older televisions could only produce 50 images per second, so dogs would only see flickering images; modern televisions are fast enough to appear as moving pictures to dogs.

271) Bill Clinton is the only president who was a Rhodes Scholar.

272) William Howard Taft was the heaviest U.S. president; he weighed about 340 pounds when he left office.

273) If you hear thunder about 15 seconds after seeing lightning, the lightning is about 3 miles away. Sound travels about one mile in five seconds.

274) Singer Johnny Mathis was a world class athlete in the high jump. He was invited to the Olympic trials when he got a recording contract; his major high jump competitor in the San Francisco Bay area where he grew up was future NBA Hall of Fame star Bill Russell.

275) 2-nonenal is the chemical thought to be responsible for old people smell; its production increases with age starting at about age 40.

276) Six presidents didn't have a wife when they took office; Jefferson, Jackson, Van Buren, and Arthur were all widowers; Cleveland married while in office; Buchanan never married.

277) The average person spends three months of their life sitting on the toilet.

278) Forty is the only number spelled out in English that has its letters in alphabetical order.

279) Guion Bluford was the first African American in space in 1983.

280) The Statue of Liberty's shoe size would be 879.

281) In 1960, Sri Lanka was the first nation to have a female prime minister.

282) Paraguay is the only country with a two-sided (different designs on each side) flag.

283) The blanket octopus has the largest size difference between males and females of any non-microscopic animal. Females are 10,000 to 40,000 times larger than males; females may be 6.5 feet in length; males are 1 inch.

284) In the second half of the 18th century to study the health effects of coffee, King Gustav III of Sweden commuted the death sentence of a pair of twins on condition that one drank three pots of coffee each day for the rest of their life, and one drank three pots of tea each day. He appointed two doctors to supervise the experiment; both doctors and the king died before the experiment was complete. The tea drinking twin died first at age 83.

285) The average American golf course consumes 312,000 gallons of water per day.

286) You need 14 calendars, seven for January 1 falling on each day of the week without a leap year and seven for January 1 falling on each day of the week with a leap year, for a perpetual calendar.

287) The word poecilonym is a synonym for synonym.

288) In 1991, the world's first webcam was created to check the status of a coffee pot at Cambridge University.

289) The Maldives is the lowest elevation country in the world; it is composed of 1,200 mostly uninhabited islands in the Indian Ocean with a maximum elevation of six feet.

290) Educated people have believed the Earth was round for about 2,500 years. Pythagoras postulated the Earth was round in the 6th century BC; Aristotle agreed is was round in the 4th century BC.

291) Bamboo is the fastest growing plant; certain species can grow three feet in a day

292) The movie *Limelight* by Charlie Chaplin had a 20-year gap between its release and winning an Oscar. It was officially released in 1952 but was not released in Los Angeles County and eligible for an Oscar until 1972. It won a Best Original Score Oscar in 1973 and is Charlie Chaplin's only competitive Oscar win.

293) Of all the people in the world who have ever lived to 65 years old, about two-thirds are alive today.

294) The word set has the most definitions of any English word; set has 464 definitions in the Oxford English dictionary; run is second at 396 definitions.

295) Philip Noel-Baker of Great Britain is the only Olympic medalist to also win a Nobel Prize. He won a silver medal in the 1500-meter run in 1920 and the Nobel Peace Prize in 1959.

296) The U.S. icon Uncle Sam was based on Samuel Wilson who during the War of 1812 was a meat packer. He supplied barrels of beef to the army stamped with "U.S." for United States, but soldiers started referring to it as Uncle Sam's.

297) The thinnest skin on the human body is the eyelid. It is 0.05 mm thick; the palms and soles of feet are the thickest at 1.5 mm.

298) Dogs have 13 blood types; humans only have four.

299) The word karaoke literally means empty orchestra.

300) Dr. Seuss wrote *Green Eggs and Ham* after his editor dared him to write a book using fewer than 50 different words.

Facts 301-600

301) According to Ernest Hemmingway, the only three sports are bullfighting, motor racing, and mountaineering, and "All the rest are merely games."

302) In 1965, Satchell Paige pitched three innings for the Kansas City Athletics against the Boston Red Sox at the age of 59.

303) When the *Mona Lisa* was stolen from the Louvre in 1911, Picasso was questioned as a suspect.

304) The Harlem Globetrotters are the only sports team to play on all seven continents.

305) Subway has the most locations worldwide of any fast food franchise.

306) Famed writers Miguel de Cervantes and William Shakespeare died on the same day, April 23, 1616.

307) *Toy Story* (1995) was the word's first computer animated feature film.

308) Napoleon Bonaparte has been portrayed more often in films than any other real person.

309) Jimmy Carter was the first president to attend Monday night football.

310) *Marty* (1955) is the only film based on a television show to win the Best Picture Oscar.

311) The asshole is the first part of the human body to form in the womb, so every human starts out as an asshole; some just stay that way.

312) *Bambi* holds the record for the longest time between an original film and its sequel; *Bambi II* was released in 2006 which was 64 years after the original.

313) Presidents Thomas Jefferson and John Adams both died on July 4, 1826.

314) The first magazine ever was launched in 1663 in Germany; it was a philosophy and literature periodical.

315) Sacagawea has more statues in her honor than anyone else in the U.S.

316) The spire on the Empire State building was meant to be used as an airship dock.

317) If not limited to the major parties, over 200 women have run for U.S. president.

318) Annapolis, Maryland and Albany, New York are the only two state capitals named for royalty. Annapolis is named for Princess Anne of Denmark and Norway who became Queen of England; Albany is named for the Duke of York and Albany who became King James II of England.

319) Daniel Day-Lewis is the only person to win the Best Actor Oscar three times for My Left Foot, *There Will Be Blood*, and *Lincoln*.

320) The United Kingdom and Great Britain are not the same; Great Britain includes England, Scotland, and Wales; the United Kingdom also includes Northern Ireland.

321) Thirteen states are entirely north of the southernmost point of Canada - Alaska, Washington, Oregon, Idaho, Montana, North Dakota,

South Dakota, Minnesota, Wisconsin, Michigan, Vermont, New Hampshire, Maine.

322) Princess Anne was the only female athlete at the 1976 summer Olympics not given a sex test.

323) Adjusted for inflation, *Home Alone* (1990) is the highest grossing comedy of all time in the U.S.

324) The movie *Romancing the Stone* centers around an American kidnapping in Colombia; ironically, an increase in American kidnappings in Colombia caused the filming to be moved to Mexico.

325) Antarctica has the largest volcanic region; there is an area of over 100 volcanoes under the ice sheet in western Antarctica.

326) There is only one species of insect native to Antarctica - the Antarctic midge.

327) Over 80 women worldwide have been elected or appointed head of their country.

328) Until the 1770s, de-crusted, moistened and balled up bread was used to erase lead pencil marks.

329) Mosquitoes like blood type O the most. They prefer it twice as much as type A; type B is their second choice.

330) McDonald's is by far the largest toy distributor in the world; about 20% of its meals are Happy Meals with a toy.

331) The Mediterranean Sea is referenced in the Bible as the Great Sea.

332) The first U.S. minimum wage was instituted in 1938 at $0.25 per hour, the equivalent of about $4.13 today.

333) The Eiffel Tower is the most visited paid monument in the world.

334) George Burns is regarded as the first television entertainer to step out of character and break the fourth wall by talking directly to the television audience on *The George Burns and Gracie Allen Show* from 1950-1958.

335) After an accident during the race, John Akhwari of Tanzania ran the last 14 miles of the marathon in the 1968 Mexico City Olympics with a dislocated knee. When asked later why he kept going, he said, "My country did not send me 9,000 miles to start the race; they sent me 9,000 miles to finish the race." He finished more than an hour behind the winner and was hailed as an Olympic hero and a symbol of the spirit of the games.

336) H.G. Wells coined the term "atomic bomb" approximately 30 years before its invention.

337) Manon Rheaume was the first woman to appear in any NHL game. She goaltended for the Tampa Bay Lightning in a pre-season game against the St. Louis Blues in September 1992.

338) In 1863, a military draft was started to provide troops for the Union army; the draft was set up to allow two ways that you could avoid going. You could pay $300 or find someone else to go in your place; what happened is that people paid $300 to have someone else go in their place. Some people made a career out of taking the money to be a substitute, deserting, and repeating the process.

339) Your glabella is the skin between the eyebrows just above the nose.

340) Solitaire is the most widely played card game in the world.

341) The Cadillac car brand was named for the founder of Detroit, Michigan; the French explorer Antoine Laumet de la Mothe, sieur de Cadillac founded Detroit in 1701.

342) Winnie the Pooh's real name is Edward Bear.

343) Aretha Franklin was the first woman inducted into the Rock and Roll Hall of Fame in 1987.

344) In psychology, the tendency for people to believe they are above average is called the Lake Wobegon effect from Garrison Keillor's *A Prairie Home Companion.*

345) Matthias was the apostle who replaced Judas Iscariot.

346) Gillis Grafstrom won a gold medal in the same event in both the Summer and Winter Olympics. He won a gold medal in the 1920 Antwerp Summer games before figure skating was moved to the Winter Olympics in 1924 where he won gold again. He also repeated as gold medalist in 1928.

347) In bowling, three strikes in a row is called a turkey because in the late 18th and early 19th century, bowling tournaments gave out food items as tournament prizes. At some point, getting three strikes in a row became associated with winning a turkey, and the name spread and stuck. Due to the much cruder equipment and lanes of long ago, getting three strikes in a row was a very difficult feat compared to today.

348) Charlton Heston has the longest screen time performance to ever win the Best Actor Oscar; he was on screen for 2 hours 1 minute and 23 seconds for *Ben-Hur* (1959).

349) The Egyptian pyramids were built by paid laborers not slaves.

350) Albert Einstein was offered the presidency of Israel in 1952 but turned it down.

351) As a republic and a state, Texas has had 12 different capital cities including Galveston, Houston, and Austin.

352) Cats are such picky eaters because they seem to be naturally driven to eat foods with about equal energy from protein and fat. They

will seek out these ratios even overriding taste preferences; science has no idea how they know what food provides the correct ratio.

353) Armadillos always gives birth to four identical offspring. A single embryo splits into four as part of their normal reproduction.

354) Under the 5th amendment to the U.S. Constitution, you can't be forced by police to unlock a phone with a password, but you can be forced to unlock it with a fingerprint. A fingerprint isn't protected under the amendment since it is something you have rather than something you know.

355) John B. Kelly Sr. won gold medals in the single and double sculls in the 1920 Antwerp Olympics and gold in the double sculls in the 1924 Paris Olympics and was the father of actress Grace Kelly who became Princess of Monaco.

356) Astoria, Oregon is the oldest city west of the Rocky Mountains; it was founded in 1811.

357) In ancient Egypt, the penalty for killing a cat even accidentally was death.

358) Greenland is part of the Kingdom of Denmark; it is so large that if you include it as part of Denmark's area, Denmark is the 12th largest country in the world.

359) South Africa is the first nation that created nuclear weapons and then voluntarily got rid of them.

360) *All in the Family* in 1971 had the first toilet heard flushing on U.S. television.

361) Golf balls were originally made of wood; in the early 17th century, wood was replaced by a feather ball which consisted of boiled feathers compressed inside a stitched leather cover.

362) The goose was the first bird domesticated by man more than 4,000 years ago in Egypt.

363) in 1935, Krueger's Finest beer became the first canned beer go on sale in the United States in Richmond, Virginia.

364) The actor who played Jethro on television's *The Beverly Hillbillies* was the son of Max Baer Sr. who was world heavyweight boxing champion in 1934.

365) The border between the United States and Mexico is the most frequently crossed international border in the world.

366) Baron Pierre de Coubertin, founder of the modern Olympics, won a gold medal at the 1912 Olympic games in mixed literature. Art competition was introduced in 1912 and continued in the Olympics through 1948; Coubertin won for a poem.

367) Annapolis, Maryland is the only state capital that was once the national capital.

368) Due to behavioral differences, men are five times more likely than women to be hit by lightning.

369) Scorpions can live up to six days without air; they can also go up to a year without eating.

370) Pronoia is the opposite of paranoia; it is a feeling that a conspiracy exists to help you.

371) William Shakespeare is the only person to have their own Dewey Decimal classification.

372) Only three people have won individual gold medals in the same event in four consecutive Olympics; they are Michael Phelps (swimming 200-meter individual medley), Carl Lewis (long jump), and Al Oerter (discus).

373) The first organ transplants occurred in 800 BC when Indian doctors performed skin grafts.

374) In pure powder form, caffeine is white.

375) Barbara Bush and Abigail Adams husbands and sons both served as U.S. president.

376) To allow visitors to travel safely to Olympia, a truce or ekecheiria was put in place before and during each of the ancient Olympic games. Wars were suspended; legal disputes were put on hold, and no death penalties were carried out during this time.

377) Denver, Colorado is named after James William Denver who is the great great grandfather of actor Bob Denver who played Gilligan on *Gilligan's Island.*

378) Your taste buds are replaced every 10-14 days.

379) Adjusted for inflation, *Waterworld* in 1995 was the first film to surpass the budget for *Cleopatra* in 1963.

380) The Statue of Liberty originally also served as a lighthouse.

381) Emma Thompson was the first person to win an Oscar for acting and writing; she won the Best Actress Oscar for *Howards End* (1992) and the Best Adapted Screenplay Oscar for *Sense and Sensibility* (1995).

382) The last man on the Moon was in 1972.

383) The black mamba is the fastest moving land snake; it can move at speeds up to 12 mph.

384) In an average lifetime, human skin completely replaces itself 900 times.

385) The horned toad squirts blood from its eyes when attacked.

386) Italy declared war on both Germany and the Allies in WWII; one month after surrendering to the allies, Italy declared war on Germany, its former ally.

387) A dog's DNA is 99.9% the same as a gray wolf.

388) Finland has the most heavy metal bands per capita.

389) Beethoven, Brahms, Chopin, Handel, Liszt, and Ravel were all bachelors.

390) President William Howard Taft had a special bathtub big enough to hold four men installed in the White House.

391) You can tell the age of a whale by counting the rings in its earwax.

392) In 1863, Venezuela was the first country to abolish capital punishment for all crimes.

393) American Eddie Eagan is the only person to win gold medals in both the winter and summer Olympics. He won for boxing in 1920 and bobsled in 1932.

394) Bears don't urinate while they hibernate. Their body converts the urine into protein, and they use it as food.

395) Before alarm clocks were invented, knocker-ups were people who would tap on client's windows with a long stick until they were awake.

396) Red is the most common color on national flags.

397) The peregrine falcon was the first animal placed on the endangered species list.

398) Linus Pauling is the only person to win two unshared Nobel Prizes.

399) Baseball Hall of Fame player Eddie Mathews was on the cover of the very first *Sports Illustrated* ever published in August 1954.

400) King James IV of Scotland paid people so that he could practice dentistry on them. He was an amateur dentist and very interested in medicine; he established the Royal College of Surgeons in Scotland two centuries before it was established in England.

401) The eruption of Mount Tambora volcano in Indonesia in 1815 is the most powerful explosion ever witnessed on Earth. It was equivalent to 800 megatons of TNT, 14 times larger than the largest man-made explosion.

402) Originally, people bowed to the U.S. president; Thomas Jefferson was the first president to shake hands rather than bowing.

403) A galactic or cosmic year is the amount of time it takes the Sun to orbit once around the center of the Milky Way Galaxy, about 230 million years.

404) Indian chief Geronimo rode in Theodore Roosevelt's inaugural parade.

405) Ronald Reagan is the only president to have been the leader of a union; he was president of the Screen Actors Guild.

406) About 5,500 WWII bombs are still discovered in Germany each year.

407) Alaska has the largest number of active volcanoes of any state; 130 out of the 169 active volcanoes in the U.S. are in Alaska.

408) Canada has a longer coastline than the rest of the world combined. At 125,567 miles, Canada's coastline is 3.5 times longer than any other country.

409) The left leg of a chicken is more tender than the right. Chickens scratch with their right leg building up more muscle in that leg and making it tougher than the left.

410) The first issue of *National Geographic* was published in 1888.

411) High heels were originally created in ancient Egypt to keep butcher's feet out of the blood. They became more popular later when Persian nobility used them when riding horses to help them stay in their stirrups.

412) Fortune cookies were invented in the United States.

413) In the television show *Have Gun - Will Travel,* the lead character's name Paladin comes from the Paladins who were the 12 knights in Charlemagne's court in the 8th century. Over time, paladin has come to mean generically a knight, warrior, or chivalrous person.

414) Until 2018, "Don't be evil" was the unofficial corporate motto of Google.

415) MLB player Joel Youngblood got two hits for two different teams in two different cities on the same day. He was traded from the Mets to the Expos on August 4, 1982; after the Mets day game, he flew to Philadelphia which was hosting the Expos for a night game.

416) About 20% of all women in London in the 1700s were prostitutes. Prostitution was a huge business generating about $2 billion annually in today's dollars.

417) The part of a sundial that casts the shadow is called a gnomon from Greek meaning indicator.

418) The St. Louis Cardinals name originally referred to the color of their uniforms and not the bird. Willie McHale, a columnist for the St. Louis Republic, overheard a woman in the stands describe the uniforms as a shade of cardinal. He began using the nickname rather than their

previous name, the Perfectos, and it caught on. The bird logo didn't appear until the 1920s.

419) The first African American was elected to serve in the U.S. Congress in 1870; he was a senator from Mississippi.

420) In the 1956 Melbourne Olympics, the equestrian events took place in Stockholm, Sweden because Australia had a strict six-month quarantine for horses entering the county and would not change it for the Olympics, so Stockholm was selected as the alternate venue for the equestrian events.

421) The average person walks about 75,000 miles in their life.

422) Before 1938, toothbrushes were made using boar hairs.

423) Morocco has the world's oldest continuously operating university; it has existed since 859 AD.

424) *Pocahontas* was the first animated Disney film to have an interracial romance.

425) In ancient Rome, it was considered a sign of leadership to be born with a crooked nose.

426) There is enough gold in the Earth's core to coat the entire surface of the Earth to a depth of 1.5 feet.

427) Giraffes have seven neck vertebrae, the same as humans.

428) Dr. Seuss was the first to use the word "nerd" in print; it is the name of a creature in *If I Ran the Zoo* published in 1950.

429) The megalodon shark is thought to be the largest shark to have ever lived. It became extinct about 2.6 million years ago and was up to 59 feet long and weighed 65 tons.

430) A fylfot is a heraldic name for the symbol that was later known as the swastika.

431) Sharks don't get cavities because the outside of their teeth is made of fluoride.

432) Cher is the oldest female artist to have a number one hit on Billboard's Hot 100 at age 52 in 1999.

433) The blue whale is the largest animal ever known to have lived on Earth. They can be up to 100 feet long and 200 tons.

434) Human babies can breathe and swallow at the same time; adults can't.

435) Hepatitis B is the most common infectious disease in the world; more than one-quarter of the world's population is infected.

436) Excluding man, dolphins have the longest tested memory. Bottlenose dolphins have unique whistles like names; studies have shown that they remember the whistle of other dolphins they have lived with even after 20 years of separation.

437) In 1992, *Malcolm X* was the first non-documentary film given permission to film in Mecca.

438) In 1952, Mr. Potato Head was the first toy advertised on U.S. television.

439) In 1977, the show *Soap* featured the first openly gay character on U.S. television.

440) Monaco is the capital of Monaco; it is both a city and a country.

441) Agatha Christie is the most widely translated author in the world.

442) Henry Ford was likely America's first billionaire in 1925. John D. Rockefeller is often cited as the first American billionaire in 1916, but his wealth was probably less than a billion at the time.

443) Argentina has the highest number of psychiatrists per capita, about six times more than the U.S.

444) By area, Lake Michigan is the largest lake entirely within the U.S.

445) The human ears and nose never stop growing.

446) The can opener was invented 45 years after tin cans were invented.

447) Iguanas have three eyes. They have a third parietal eye on top of their head that can just distinguish light and dark.

448) Bullwinkle Moose is originally from Moosylvania; it is a small island in Lake of the Woods that neither the U.S. nor Canada wants to claim.

449) Over 2,300 years ago, Hippocrates described walking as "man's best medicine."

450) The frisbee was originally called the Pluto Platter.

451) Florida is the flattest state; there is only 345 feet between its highest and lowest elevations.

452) In 1931, female pitcher Jackie Mitchell became the first woman in professional baseball to strikeout Babe Ruth and Lou Gehrig. In an exhibition game between the New York Yankees and the Chattanooga Lookouts, a class AA minor league team, she struck out Ruth and Gehrig in succession; she was 17 years old at the time. Baseball commissioner Kenesaw Mountain Landis banned women from the sport later that year.

453) At age 59, Sean Connery is the oldest man to win *People* magazine's sexiest man alive.

454) Australia has the highest gambling rate in the world; over 80% of adults gamble in some form.

455) Twelve American prisoners of war were killed in the Hiroshima atomic bomb blast.

456) Saffron is made from crocus flowers; only the stigma part of the flower is used. It takes 70,000 to 250,000 flowers to make one pound of saffron which is why it is so expensive.

457) A newborn human baby has about one cup of blood in their body.

458) The movie *Ben-Hur* is based on a novel by an American Civil War general who was also governor of the New Mexico Territory. Lew Wallace published *Ben-Hur: A Tale of the Christ* in 1880; it was the all-time best-selling novel in the U.S. until the publication of Gone with the Wind in 1936.

459) Aluminum is the major constituent of rubies.

460) Iran has the highest rate of cosmetic nose surgery.

461) Boxing was the first sport to be filmed in 1894.

462) At age 48, George Blanda is the oldest player ever in an NFL game.

463) Chocolate is the only edible substance that melts just below human body temperature. Chocolate melts at 93 degrees which is why it melts in your mouth.

464) German chocolate cake originated in the United States; it was named after American baker Samuel German.

465) British mathematician Charles Lutwidge Dodgson is better known as Lewis Carroll, author of *Alice's Adventures in Wonderland.*

466) President Gerald Ford was once a fashion model; he worked for *Cosmopolitan* and *Look* magazines in the 1940s.

467) Adjusted for inflation, *Snow White and the Seven Dwarfs* (1937) is the earliest movie made that has grossed $1 billion in the U.S.

468) If you pay a kidnapping ransom in the United States, you can deduct it on your taxes.

469) Christopher Cross is the only artist to win best new artist and record, album, and song of the year Grammys in the same year in 1981. Adele is the only other artist to win all four awards, but she didn't win them in the same year.

470) Notre Dame Cathedral was almost demolished in the 19th century but was saved by Victor Hugo's *The Hunchback of Notre Dame*; Hugo wrote the novel partially to save the cathedral from demolition.

471) The clavicle or collar bone is the most frequently broken bone in the human body.

472) At age 29, Adrien Brody is the youngest Best Actor Oscar winner for *The Pianist* (2002).

473) Research has shown that most mammals on average live for about 1.5 billion heartbeats. Larger animals have slower heartbeats, so they live longer; humans used to fit the pattern but with health and medical improvements, we last longer than our size predicts. At 60 beats per minute, 1.5 billion heartbeats would be 47.5 years.

474) The "DC" in DC Comics stands for Detective Comics.

475) The king cobra is the only snake that builds a nest. They can lay up to 40 eggs at once; the nest is built from vegetation and helps keep the eggs safe.

476) The word orchid is Greek and literally means testicle.

477) The Earth orbits around the Sun at 66,600 mph.

478) Grey whales always mate in a threesome with two males and one female; one of the males is dominant and the other assists.

479) St. Augustine, Florida is the oldest city in the U.S.; it was founded in 1565.

480) The heat of a bolt of lightning is about five times hotter than the surface of the Sun.

481) The constitutions of seven states still specifically ban atheists from holding public office. The states are Arkansas, Maryland, Mississippi, North Caroline, South Carolina, Tennessee, and Texas.

482) Vatican City drinks more wine per person than any other country. They consume about 74 liters per person annually, more than seven times more than the U.S.

483) Malaria is believed to have killed more people than any other disease throughout history; it still kills about 1 million people annually.

484) James Madison was the shortest president at 5'4".

485) The whale shark has the world's largest egg at up to 12 inches long; the ostrich has the largest laid egg.

486) The Seattle Metropolitans were the first U.S. hockey team to win the Stanley Cup in 1917. The next season the National Hockey Association was replaced by the NHL; the Stanley Cup was first awarded in 1893.

487) Men wore high heels before women did; it was a sign of status. In the 1600's, women started to wear high heels as a way of appropriating masculine power; it then filtered down to the lower classes. Men eventually quit wearing high heels when it was no longer a power symbol.

488) Liza Minnelli is the only Oscar winner whose parents were both Oscar winners; her parents are Vincent Minnelli and Judy Garland.

489) In 5 BC, Rome was the first city to reach a population of 1 million people.

490) Great Smoky Mountains is the most visited U.S. National Park.

491) Queen Elizabeth II served as a mechanic and driver in WWII.

492) The first email was sent in 1971.

493) Lucille Ball was the first woman to run a major television studio. She ran Desilu Studio starting in 1962; the studio produced many popular shows including *Mission Impossible* and *Star Trek*.

494) Belgium invented French fried potatoes in the late 17th century.

495) Adolf Hitler was Roman Catholic.

496) The Barbie doll's full name is Barbara Millicent Roberts.

497) The world's most popular first name is Mohammed and its variations.

498) Australia has the world's largest feral camel herd, as many as 1 million camels at one point. They were imported in the 19th century, and many were later set free as the automobile took over; they now roam freely with no natural predators.

499) Amen means "So be it" in Hebrew.

500) In 1950, Diners Club was the first universal credit card that could be used at a variety of places.

501) Sleeping on the job is acceptable in Japan because it is viewed as exhaustion from working hard.

502) A googolplexian is the largest named number. A googol is one followed by 100 zeroes; a googolplex is one followed by a googol of zeroes; a googolplexian is one followed by a googolplex of zeroes.

503) The population density of ancient Rome was about eight times greater than modern New York City.

504) Fred Flintstone's "yabba-dabba-doo" was inspired by Brylcreem's "A little dab'll do you." The mother of the actor who voiced Fred Flintstone liked to say the Brylcreem slogan, so he suggested it to the creators.

505) *Bambi* was the first Disney film without human characters.

506) The NHL didn't allow goalies to drop to the ice to make saves until 1917. Prior to this, goaltenders were required to remain standing.

507) Published in 1852, *Uncle Tom's Cabin* was the first American novel to sell 1 million copies.

508) The kori bustard is the heaviest bird capable of flight. They are from Africa and can weigh 40 pounds.

509) A group of bears is called a sloth.

510) Prior to *The Artist* in 2011, *The Apartment* (1960) was the last entirely black and white movie to win the Best Picture Oscar. *Schindler's List* in 1993 had color in some scenes.

511) In 1951, Bernie Geoffrion was the first NHL player to use a slapshot.

512) The tortoise is the longest living land animal of any kind; the oldest known lived to 250.

513) As soon as sand tiger shark embryos develop teeth while still in the womb, the largest of the embryos in each of the two uteruses attacks and eats its siblings leaving just two pups to be born.

514) The theme music for television's *Monty Python's Flying Circus* was written by John Philip Sousa; it is "The Liberty Bell March."

515) Ambisinistrous means no good with either hand; it is the opposite of ambidextrous.

516) Arabic numerals were first used in India.

517) Only one person in modern recorded history has been struck dead by a meteorite. In 2016 in India, a 40-year-old man was relaxing outside on the grounds of a small engineering college when there was the sound of an explosion; he was found next to a two-foot crater and later succumbed to injuries sustained.

518) William Howard Taft is the only man to have been both Chief Justice of the U.S. Supreme Court and U.S. president.

519) The hyoid bone in the throat is the only bone in the human body that isn't attached to any other bone.

520) Monaco's orchestra is bigger than its army.

521) Based on land area, Jacksonville, Florida is the largest city in the 48 contiguous states at 758 square miles.

522) Tony Bennet is the oldest living artist to have a song on Billboard's Hot 100 at age 85 in 2011.

523) A cat's jaw can't move sideways, so they can't chew large chunks.

524) There are 42 eyes in a deck of 52 cards. The jack of hearts, jack of spades, and king of diamonds are in profile with only one eye showing.

525) Virginia is the most common U.S. president birth state with eight presidents.

526) The odds against any person becoming a saint are 20 million to 1.

527) Four people have won two Nobel prizes - Marie Curie, Linus Pauling, John Bardeen, and Frederick Sanger.

528) Aristarchus of Samos first proposed that the Sun was the center around which the planets orbit in the 3rd century BC; Copernicus developed a fully predictive model in the 16th century but wasn't the first to propose the concept.

529) The Monday before and the Wednesday after the MLB All-Star game are the only two days during the year where there are no MLB, NFL, NHL or NBA games played. The MLB All-Star game is always played on a Tuesday, and there are no MLB games the day before or after, and MLB is the only professional sport played in July.

530) English has more words than any other language.

531) Mary Edwards Walker is the only woman ever awarded the U.S. medal of honor; she received it for her service in the Civil War. She was a surgeon at a temporary Washington, D.C. hospital and was captured and arrested as a spy after crossing enemy lines to treat wounded civilians.

532) At the closest point, Europe and Africa are separated by nine miles between Spain and Morocco.

533) Oscar the Grouch from television's *Sesame Street* was originally orange.

534) Elena Cornaro Piscopia was the first woman in the world to receive a PhD degree in 1678 in Italy.

535) If you search for the word askew in Google, the content comes back tilted to the right.

536) New Zealand was undiscovered and devoid of humans up until 800 years ago.

537) Cleopatra was the last Pharaoh of Egypt.

538) From the Middle Ages until 1809, Finland was part of Sweden.

539) The average person spends about six years of their life dreaming.

540) In 1893, Thomas Edison built the world's first film studio.

541) Insecticides were the first product sold in aerosol spray cans.

542) The most common time to wake up in the middle of the night is 3:44 am.

543) Eleanor Roosevelt was the editor of the magazine *Babies Just Babies* when her husband was elected president.

544) The United States, Liberia, and Myanmar are the only three countries that don't use the metric system.

545) The average lightning bolt is about five miles long and one inch wide.

546) Rin Tin Tin is often credited with saving Warner Brothers Studio from bankruptcy and received the most votes for the Best Actor Oscar at the first Academy Awards in 1929 before being eliminated from the ballot. The Academy wanted to appear more serious and have a human win, so they removed him from the ballot and voted again.

547) Camels have three eyelids to protect them from sand.

548) Hotfoot Teddy was the original name of Smokey the Bear.

549) Harper Lee, author of *To Kill a Mockingbird*, was Truman Capote's best friend and next-door neighbor that he first met when he was 5 years old.

550) In 1947, *Mary Kay and Johnny* was the first U.S. television series to ever show a couple sharing a bed; it was the first sitcom in the U.S. Couples weren't shown sharing the same bed again until the 1960s.

551) Tooth enamel is the hardest substance in the human body.

552) In 1939, Earl Wild was the first pianist to give a recital on U.S. television; in 1997, he was also the first person to stream a piano performance over the internet.

553) On average, the Moon is 238,900 miles from the Earth.

554) John Cazale is the only actor to appear in multiple films and have every one nominated for the Best Picture Oscar; he appeared in *The Godfather*, *The Conversation*, *The Godfather Part II*, *Dog Day Afternoon*, and *The Deer Hunter*.

555) The first cell phone call was made in 1973.

556) The average chocolate bar has eight insect parts.

557) Lake Kinnernet is known as the Sea of Galilee in the Bible.

558) Humans, killer whales, and short finned pilot whales are the only animal species known to go through menopause.

559) Joseph A. Walker was the first person to fly into space twice; he did it in 1963 aboard an X-15 winged aircraft. Space is defined as 100 km or 62 miles above the Earth.

560) During the U.S. Civil War, women were prohibited from enlisting in both the Union and Confederate armies, but more than 600 women dressed as men joined the war anyway.

561) Kenyon College won the NCAA Division III men's swimming and diving championship for 31 consecutive years from 1980-2010. It is the most consecutive national championships for any men's or women's team in any NCAA division.

562) Less than a year before Abraham Lincoln was assassinated, his oldest son Robert was saved from being hit by a train by Edwin Booth, the brother of John Wilkes Booth.

563) Hydrogen is the most abundant element in the universe; it accounts for about 75% of the universe's mass.

564) Australia is the only country with all 10 of the deadliest snakes in the world.

565) Mexico City has the largest taxi fleet of any city in the world; it has over 140,000 taxis.

566) The Snickers candy bar is named after the creator's horse.

567) A snail's reproductive organs are in its head.

568) The book and movie title *Fahrenheit 451* are from the temperature at which book paper catches fire and burns.

569) Almost half the gold ever mined has come from Witwatersrand, South Africa.

570) At age 21, Marlee Matlin is the youngest Best Actress Oscar winner for *Children of a Lesser God* (1986).

571) Of all the text information stored on the world's computers, 80% is in English.

572) *Oliver!* in 1968 is the only G-rated movie to win the Best Picture Oscar.

573) In the original script for *Back to the Future*, the time machine wasn't a DeLorean; it was a refrigerator.

574) Rhythms is the longest common English word without any vowels.

575) Human life expectancy has increased more in the last 50 years than it has in the prior 200,000 years.

576) The word scientist was first used in 1833.

577) Israel has the highest number of museums per capita of any country.

578) A cricket's ears are located on its front legs.

579) A giraffe cleans its ears with its tongue.

580) Queen Elizabeth II is the largest landowner in the world; she technically owns 6.6 billion acres or about one-sixth of the world's land including Canada and Australia.

581) Each year, 15,000 to 18,000 new animal species are discovered; about half are insects.

582) Washington, D.C. has a smaller percent of the country's population than any other national capital in the world; it has just 0.21% of the U.S. population.

583) You could fit 1.3 million Earths inside the Sun which is an average size star.

584) Russia is the third closest country to the U.S.

585) Horseshoe crab blood is worth $14,000 per quart because of its unique chemical properties that make it very valuable in the health care industry for bacterial testing. It can coagulate around as little as one part in a trillion of bacterial contamination, and the reaction only takes 45 minutes instead of two days with mammalian blood.

586) The Montreal Canadiens NHL team is known to their fans as the Habs because Tex Rickard who owned Madison Square Garden told a reporter in 1924 that the "H" on their jersey stood for "Habitants" from the French "Les Habitants" for the early French settlers in Canada which was shortened to Habs. The "H" on their jersey really stands for hockey from "Club de Hockey Canadien."

587) Deaf-mute player William Hoy inspired the non-verbal signs used in baseball and stole over 600 bases in his career; he started his career in 1888.

588) Walter and John Huston were the first father and son to win Oscars for the same film in *The Treasure of the Sierra Madre*.

589) River and Joaquin Phoenix are the only brothers to receive acting Oscar nominations.

590) The Antarctic ice sheet has 90% of the Earth's fresh water; it is equivalent to about 230 feet of water in the world's oceans.

591) The human eye can differentiate more shades of green than any other color; that is why night vision goggles are green.

592) At age 42, Theodore Roosevelt is the youngest ever U.S. president; John F. Kennedy is the youngest elected president at age 43.

593) Leeches have 32 brains; each controls a different segment of their body.

594) In 1841, Oberlin College was the first U.S. college to confer degrees on women.

595) The whip was the first man made object to break the sound barrier. The crack a whip makes is due to a small sonic boom from breaking the sound barrier.

596) Gerald Ford lived the longest of any U.S. president at 93; Ronald Reagan was also 93 but 45 days younger.

597) The *American Gothic* painting by Grant Wood depicts his sister and his dentist.

598) Because he was afraid of flying, Cassius Clay (Muhammad Ali) wore a parachute on his flight to Rome for the 1960 Olympics.

599) The most commonly spoken word in the world is OK.

600) The U.S. film industry relocated from New York to Los Angeles in large part because of Thomas Edison who held many of the patents on the production and showing of movies and controlled the industry; film makers escaped to Los Angeles to get away from his control.

Facts 601-900

601) William Henry Harrison had the shortest term as U.S. president at just 31 days; he caught a cold on inauguration day that turned into a fatal case of pneumonia. His grandson Benjamin would later also be president.

602) Before unifying Italy, Giuseppe Garibaldi was a spaghetti salesman in Uruguay.

603) Adjusted for inflation, *The Exorcist* (1973) is the highest grossing R-rated movie of all time in the U.S.

604) Park is the most popular street name in the U.S.

605) The sperm whale produces the loudest sound of any animal. It can reach 230 decibels; a rock concert is 150 decibels.

606) Gene Autry is the only person with a star in each of the five categories (movies, television, music, radio, live performance) on the Hollywood Walk of Fame.

607) In 1457, King James II of Scotland banned golf and soccer because they interfered with archery practice needed for national defense.

608) Richard Nixon was the first president to visit all 50 states.

609) Detartrated is the longest palindrome word in English; palindromes are the same forwards and backwards.

610) A polar bear can swim 60 miles without stopping.

611) Pork is the most widely eaten meat in the world; poultry is second; beef is third.

612) In 1891, Whitcomb Judson invented the zipper for fastening shoes.

613) The tallest tsunami wave ever recorded was in Lituya Bay, Alaska in 1958; it was 1,720 feet tall. An 8.0 earthquake dropped 40 to 50 million cubic yards of rock and ice 3,000 feet down into the bay creating the wave.

614) Squidgers are the larger discs used to shoot the winks in tiddlywinks.

615) China has the most countries or territories bordering it with 14 countries and 2 territories.

616) Michigan has the highest percent of its area that is water of any state at 41.5%.

617) In its natural form, aspirin comes from the bark of the white willow tree.

618) Phoenix, Arizona has the largest population of any state capital.

619) Mexican War hero Zachary Taylor was the first man with no political experience to be elected president.

620) The term "sweat like a pig" comes from the iron smelting process and has nothing to do with pigs sweating. During the process, molten iron was poured into molds with ingots branching off a central channel which reminded people of piglets suckling on a sow, so the iron became known as pig iron. When the pig iron was cool enough to transport, it would sweat from condensation from the air giving the term "sweat like a pig."

621) Sylvester Stallone was so poor at one point that he sold his dog for $50 only to buy it back for $3,000 one week later when he sold the script for *Rocky*.

622) Playwright Tennessee Williams choked to death on the cap of a bottle of barbiturates.

623) Bananas are the most widely eaten fruit in the U.S.; apples are second.

624) Four state capitals are named after presidents – Lincoln, Jefferson City, Jackson, Madison.

625) As referenced in the Bible, myrrh is a gum resin from trees.

626) The sport of cricket originated the term hat trick. The term first appeared in 1858 in cricket where H. H. Stephenson took three wickets with three consecutive balls; fans held a collection for him and presented him with a hat bought with the proceeds.

627) *Rocky*, *Chariots of Fire*, and *Million Dollar Baby* are the only three sports related movies that have won the Best Picture Oscar.

628) Based on AKC registrations, the three most popular purebred dogs in the U.S. are the Labrador Retriever, German Shepherd, and Golden Retriever.

629) On average, most people have fewer friends than their friends have; this is known as the friendship paradox. You are more likely to be friends with someone who has more friends than someone who has fewer friends.

630) The Great Pyramid of Giza has eight sides; each of the four sides are split from base to tip by slight concave indentations creating eight sides. The indentations were first noticed by a pilot flying over in 1940.

631) Instead of toilet paper, ancient Romans used a sponge on a stick. It was shared with everyone in communal bathrooms and was kept in a bucket of heavily salted seawater.

632) Cartoon character Elmer Fudd was originally called Egghead.

633) According to Wurlitzer, the most popular jukebox song of all time is "Hound Dog" by Elvis Presley.

634) The initials "B.B." in B.B. King's name stand for Blues Boy.

635) Eight people took refuge on Noah's ark, Noah and his wife and his three sons and their wives.

636) Donald Trump was the inspiration for the character of Biff Tannen, the bully in the movie *Back to the Future*.

637) Scientists believe that herrings use farts to communicate. Herrings have excellent hearing, and their farts produce a high-pitched sound. The farts aren't from flatulence but from gulping air at the surface and storing it in their swim bladder.

638) U.S. First lady Eleanor Roosevelt refused secret service coverage and was given her own gun.

639) *My Big Fat Greek Wedding* (2002) is the highest grossing romantic comedy of all time.

640) William Howard Taft was the first president to use the Oval Office; he made the West Wing a permanent building and had the Oval Office built.

641) Grover Cleveland is the only president to serve two nonconsecutive terms; he was the 22nd and 24th president.

642) Theodore Roosevelt was the first president to leave the U.S. while in office; he went to Panama to inspect construction of the canal.

643) James Dean only made three films – *Rebel Without a Cause*, *East of Eden*, and *Giant*.

644) Mexico has the highest annual average hours worked in the world.

645) The main reason for the character layout of the qwerty keyboard we use today is to prevent typewriter jams by placing often used keys further apart.

646) Cats have more than 100 vocal sounds while dogs only have about 10.

647) Ulaanbaatar, Mongolia is the coldest national capital city in the world; winter temperatures of -40 degrees Fahrenheit are not unusual.

648) In 1984, Linda Hunt won a Best Supporting Actress Oscar for *The Year of Living Dangerously*; it was the first Oscar ever for playing the opposite sex.

649) A human can live up to 11 days without sleeping.

650) The only U.S. soil that Japan occupied during WWII were two remote Aleutian Islands; the U.S. battled Japan to retake the islands between June 1942 and August 1943.

651) U.S. President John Tyler had 15 children by two different wives.

652) Bob Fitzsimmons was the lightest boxer to ever hold the world heavyweight title; he was 167 pounds when he won the title in 1897.

653) Lebanon is the only Middle Eastern country without a desert.

654) Uzbekistan and Liechtenstein are the only two countries completely surrounded by landlocked countries.

655) Time is the most commonly used noun in the English language.

656) Of cities of 1 million or more population, Auckland, New Zealand is furthest away from another city of 1 million population or more; it is 1,347 miles away from Sydney Australia.

657) George Washington and James Monroe are the only two men who have run effectively unopposed for U.S. president.

658) *Dumbo* was the first Disney animated feature film set in America.

659) In Disney's *Snow White and the Seven Dwarfs*, Snow White is 14 years old.

660) Ecuador is the only point on the equator with snow on the ground.

661) Maine is the closest state to Africa; Quoddy Head, Maine is 3,154 miles from Morocco. It is almost 1,000 miles closer than Florida.

662) The project that would become the Statue of Liberty was originally conceived of as a peasant Muslim woman in traditional dress. The statue was originally intended for Egypt before they turned the project down, and it was redesigned for the U.S.

663) Israel is the only country in the world to have a net gain of trees in the last 100 years.

664) If you weigh 150 pounds on Earth, you would weigh 4,200 pounds on the Sun.

665) The duffel bag gets its name from Duffel, Belgium where the thick cloth used to make the bag originated.

666) Women spend about one year of their life deciding what to wear.

667) Mexico has the most emigrants, people living in other countries.

668) Adult domestic cats only meow to communicate with humans. They don't meow to each other; it is thought to be a post-domestication extension of kittens mewing.

669) Fidelity, bravery, integrity is the FBI's motto.

670) In 1916, Germany was the first country to implement daylight saving time to save energy during WWI.

671) *The Artist* (2011) from France was the first movie from a non-English speaking country to win the Best Picture Oscar.

672) The worldwide literacy rate is 86.3%.

673) The locust is the only insect considered kosher.

674) A human fart travels about 10 feet per second or 7 mph.

675) Hollywood star Clark Gable was the inspiration for Bugs Bunny.

676) Calvin Coolidge is the only president born on the 4th of July.

677) A group of cats is called a clowder.

678) In 1861, the *Times of London* carried the world's first weather forecast.

679) Ninety percent of all meteorites ever found come from Antarctica.

680) The average cumulus cloud weighs 1.1 million pounds.

681) President Andrew Jackson was shot at twice at point-blank range but survived because both guns misfired; it was the first assassination attempt against a U.S. president.

682) Piggy banks got their name because they were originally made from pygg clay. The clay was used to make bowls and jars and other containers that people started to store change in; the containers were not made into pig shapes until much later.

683) Atlanta, Georgia is the world's busiest airport based on passenger traffic.

684) Johann Sebastian Bach enjoyed coffee so much that he wrote a cantata for it.

685) Johnny Vander Meer is the only pitcher in Major League Baseball history to throw consecutive no hitters. He did it for the 1938 Cincinnati Reds.

686) Hong Kong has more skyscrapers than any other city in the world; New York City is second; Dubai is third. There is no exact definition of a skyscraper, but they are generally considered to be 150 meters or taller.

687) The Cookie Monster's real name on *Sesame Street* is Sid.

688) Charlie Chaplin has been portrayed more times on the screen by other actors than any other actor.

689) At the 1988 Calgary Olympics, officials were so concerned about Mexican cross-country skier Roberto Alvarez during the 50 km race that they sent out a search party. He had never skied more than 20 km, and officials thought he was lost or injured; he finished more than an hour behind the second to last place finisher.

690) Dwight D. Eisenhower was the first president to govern over all 50 states.

691) It is illegal for drug companies to advertise directly to consumers almost everywhere in the world except the United States and New Zealand.

692) President James Buchanan was morally opposed to slavery but believed it was protected by the constitution, so he bought slaves with his own money and freed them.

693) The lens of the eye continues to grow throughout a person's life.

694) North Dakota is the geographic center of North America.

695) Leann Rimes is the youngest solo singer ever to win a Grammy at age 13.

696) The shortest complete English sentence is "Go."

697) When accused of being two-faced, Abraham Lincoln said "If I had two faces, would I be wearing this one?"

698) Q is the least used letter in the English alphabet.

699) Of all the animal species scientists have studied, domestic cats are the only one that shows no outward signs of conciliatory behavior.

700) Author James Patterson has the most entries on the *New York Times* best-seller list.

701) The highest percentage of Americans are awake at 6:00 pm, about 97.5%.

702) Andrew Johnson is the only president who made his own clothes; he had been a tailor's apprentice and opened his own tailor shop. He made his own clothes most of his life.

703) The U.S. $10,000 bill was last printed in 1945 and is the largest denomination ever in public circulation; Salmon P. Chase, Secretary of the Treasury, had his portrait on it.

704) The V-shaped formation of a flock of geese is called a skein.

705) A rhinoceros' horn is made of hair.

706) "Happy Birthday to You" was originally called "Good Morning to All" before the words were changed, and it was published in 1935.

707) There were eight U.S. national capital cities before Washington, D.C. - Philadelphia, Pennsylvania; Baltimore, Maryland; Lancaster

Pennsylvania; York, Pennsylvania; Princeton, New Jersey; Annapolis, Maryland; Trenton, New Jersey; and New York City.

708) According to the *Guinness Book of World Records*, Scientology founder L. Ron Hubbard has the most published works for any single author with 1,084.

709) Disc jockey Alan Freed is generally given credit for coining the term "rock and roll."

710) Science Nobel Prize winners are 22 times more likely than their peers to have performed as actors, dancers, or magicians during their lives.

711) Israel has the highest per capita consumption of turkey.

712) Papua New Guinea has the largest number of languages spoken of any country; it has about 850 languages, one for every 8,000 citizens.

713) Missouri and Tennessee share the most borders with other states; each border eight other states.

714) The term "slush fund" was originally used by sailors to refer to the side money they made selling animal fat; sailors sold the fat or grease from the meat cooked on board to tallow makers.

715) *Ben-Hur* is the only Hollywood film to make the Vatican's approved list in the religious category.

716) Peter the Great ordered the Russian nobility to become more European by shaving off their beards.

717) In the 1961-62 NBA season, Wilt Chamberlain averaged more minutes per game than there are minutes in a game. He played every minute of the 80-game season, and with overtime games, he ended up averaging 48.5 minutes played per game.

718) The sperm whale dives deeper and stays underwater longer than any other whale. They can dive for more than an hour and more than 4,000 feet deep.

719) Blue whales can consume 500,000 calories in a single mouthful feeding on krill.

720) France and its territories cover more time zones than any other country. France has 12 times zones; the U.S. and Russia and their territories each cover 11 time zones.

721) Rutgers and Princeton played in the first college football game. In 1869, Rutgers beat Princeton 6-4 in a game that had 25 players on each side and one-point touchdowns; the first team to reach six points was declared the winner.

722) After man, the longest living land mammal is the elephant; the oldest known lived to 86.

723) Mozart wrote numerous letters and an entire song focused on poop; no one is quite sure if it was just his odd humor or a mental issue.

724) Scarlett O'Hara's real first name in *Gone with the Wind* is Katie; Scarlett is her middle name.

725) The sailfish is the fastest fish with speeds up to 68 mph.

726) Almost one-third of the world's languages are only spoken in Africa.

727) The word goodbye is a contraction of "God be with ye."

728) The greatest distance on Earth between the nearest points of land is 994 miles from Bouvet Island in the South Atlantic to Antarctica.

729) The cockroach is possibly the largest methane producer relative to its body size; they emit up to 43 times their weight in methane annually.

730) The human eye can distinguish about 10 million colors.

731) Windsor Castle employs a fendersmith who just tends and lights fires.

732) All the gold ever mined would fit in four Olympic swimming pools.

733) William Howard Taft was the last president with facial hair.

734) In the James Bond films, the acronym SPECTRE stands for Special Executive for Counterintelligence Terror Revenge and Extortion.

735) San Marino has the oldest surviving constitution in the world dating to 1600; the U.S. constitution is the second oldest.

736) Gallaudet University, a school for the deaf, originated the football huddle in 1892. They huddled to avoid the other team seeing their sign language.

737) Luise Rainer and Katharine Hepburn are the only two actresses who have won consecutive Best Actress Oscars. Luise Rainer won for *The Great Ziegfeld* (1936) and *The Good Earth* (1937); Katharine Hepburn won for *Guess Who's Coming to Dinner* (1967) and *The Lion in Winter* (1968).

738) Benjamin Franklin wrote a collection of essays titled *Fart Proudly*.

739) John Quincy Adams served in the U.S. House of Representatives after he served as president.

740) John Tyler was the first vice president to become president upon the death of a president; he succeeded William Henry Harrison who died of pneumonia 31 days into his presidency.

741) Melania Trump, Michelle Obama, and Eleanor Roosevelt are tied as the tallest U.S. first ladies at 5'11".

742) In the original book *The Wonderful Wizard of Oz*, Dorothy's slippers are silver not ruby.

743) Osmium is the densest naturally occurring element; it is about 25 times denser than water.

744) The longest tennis rally (a single point) ever recorded in professional tennis lasted 643 shots. It took 29 minutes for the single point in a 1984 women's tournament.

745) A rat can fall 50 feet uninjured.

746) The first nationally televised football game was in 1934 on Thanksgiving Day with Detroit playing Chicago.

747) Australia has the largest population of poisonous snakes of any country.

748) George Washington and Benjamin Franklin appeared on the first U.S. postage stamps issued in 1847.

749) The character of the boy Dill Harris who is visiting for the summer in *To Kill a Mockingbird* is based on author Truman Capote. He was a childhood friend and neighbor of author Harper Lee, and they remained lifelong friends.

750) Russia has 11 time zones; it spans over 5,700 miles east to west.

751) The Who is the only band to play at both Woodstock and Live Aid.

752) Denmark has the world's oldest operating amusement park; it started in 1583.

753) The Canary Islands are named after dogs. When the first Europeans arrived, they found large dogs on Grand Canary; canaria is the Latin word for dog.

754) In Victorian London, people were paid to collect dog poop for use in tanning leather.

755) The largest national park in the world is in Greenland. The Northeast Greenland National Park is 375,000 square miles; it is about 100 times bigger than Yellowstone National Park and only has about 500 visitors per year.

756) A day on Mars is 40 minutes longer than a day on Earth.

757) Japan and Russia still haven't officially signed a peace treaty between them ending WWII; they have a dispute over the Kuril Islands.

758) Plato first wrote about the lost civilization of Atlantis in 360 BC.

759) A blue moon is defined as the second full moon in a calendar month. It happens about every three years giving the expression "once in a blue moon" for something that doesn't occur very often.

760) The Italian word vermicelli literally means little worms.

761) During WWI, the British tried to train seagulls to poop on the periscopes of enemy submarines.

762) The ancient Romans threw walnuts at weddings; they signified hoped for fertility of the bride.

763) In terms of production volume, tomatoes are the most popular fruit in the world.

764) Prior to the 20th century, lobster was considered a mark of poverty and used for fertilizer and fed to slaves. Its reputation changed

when modern transportation allowed shipping live lobsters to urban centers.

765) At President Andrew Jackson's funeral in 1845, his pet parrot was removed for swearing.

766) The fastest human sense in terms of how long it takes to process the input is hearing; it takes as little as 0.05 seconds to process.

767) When Lord Byron became a student at Cambridge, dogs were prohibited, so he got a bear as a pet. The bear stayed in his lodgings, and Byron would take him for walks around the grounds.

768) At 5,525 miles, the United States and Canada share the longest land border in the world.

769) Sapphire is the second hardest gem after diamond.

770) As originally written, Aladdin is Chinese.

771) The Volkswagen Beetle debuted in 1938. Its concept and functional objectives were formulated by Adolf Hitler, and it was designed by Ferdinand Porsche.

772) Kopi Luwak is a very expensive type of coffee known as civet coffee; it is made from partially digested coffee cherries eaten and defecated by civet cats.

773) The seahorse and pipefish are the only two species of fish where the male gives birth.

774) A blue whale's pulse is 8-10 beats per minute.

775) Green is the first color mentioned in the Bible. Genesis 1:30 states, "To every thing that creepeth upon the earth, wherein there is life, I have given every green herb for meat: and it was so."

776) Italy has won the Best Foreign Language Film Oscar the most times of any country.

777) Richard Rogers and Marvin Hamlisch are the only two people ever to win an Oscar, Emmy, Tony, Grammy, and Pulitzer.

778) Texas has the most counties of any state with 254.

779) Sphenopalatine ganglioneuralgia is the medical term for brain freeze or ice cream headache.

780) Prince Charles was the first member of the British royal family to ever graduate from university.

781) *Who Framed Roger Rabbit* (1988) is the only film where cartoon characters from Walt Disney and Warner Brothers appear together.

782) Indonesia has the most earthquakes of any country; Japan has the second most.

783) The lifespan of a housefly is 15-30 days depending on conditions.

784) President Gerald Ford was born as Leslie Lynch King Jr.; after his mother remarried, he was adopted by his stepfather.

785) Graham Hill from Great Britain is the first driver to ever complete the Triple Crown of Motorsport consisting of winning the Indianapolis 500, 24 Hours of Le Mans, and the Monaco Grand Prix over a career. He won the 1963 Monaco Grand Prix, 1966 Indianapolis 500, and 1972 Le Mans.

786) George Washington, John Adams, and Thomas Jefferson were all avid collectors and players of marbles.

787) The Amazon is the widest river in the world; it is almost 25 miles wide during the wet season.

788) During the 18th century, you could pay for your admission to the London zoo by bringing a cat or dog to feed the lions.

789) Benjamin Franklin was carried to the Constitutional Convention in a sedan chair carried by prisoners.

790) Greece invented cheesecake.

791) Bob Dylan is the only person ever to win a Nobel Prize, Pulitzer, Oscar, and Grammy.

792) Q is the only letter that doesn't appear in any state name.

793) Bamboo Harvester was the real name of television's Mister Ed.

794) The earliest pillows date back 9,000 years to Mesopotamia; they were made from stone with a curved top and were designed to keep the head off the ground and prevent insects from crawling into the mouth, nose, and ears.

795) The pineal gland in the center of the brain is the smallest organ in the human body; it is about the size of a grain of rice.

796) Danny Ainge is the only person to be named a first team high school All-American in football, basketball, and baseball. He went to high school in Eugene, Oregon and went on to play professional baseball for the Toronto Blue Jays and won two NBA championships with the Boston Celtics.

797) The ostrich is the largest bird in the world; the second largest is the southern cassowary which lives in the tropical rainforests of Indonesia, New Guinea, and the islands of northern Australia. It averages about 100 pounds compared to 230 pounds for the ostrich.

798) At 243 Earth days, Venus has the longest day of any planet in our solar system.

799) At the 1908 London Olympics, Italian Dorando Pietri was the first marathon runner to cross the finish line, but he was disqualified because he collapsed from exhaustion while finishing in the stadium and was helped up and essentially carried across the line by officials.

800) At 2,700 miles, Alaska is the widest state from east to west.

801) The highest surface wind speed ever recorded on Earth was at Mount Washington, New Hampshire with a 231-mph wind.

802) James Earl Jones was the first celebrity to make a guest appearance on *Sesame Street*; he appeared on the show's second episode.

803) Picasso used house paint in his paintings.

804) Before devoting his life to philosophy, Socrates was a mason or stone cutter.

805) An oniomaniac is obsessed with shopping.

806) *Tom Jones* was the last film John F. Kennedy saw before his assassination.

807) Elton John has performed more concerts in Madison Square Garden than any other artist.

808) Switzerland and Vatican City are the only two countries with square flags.

809) Actor Franklyn Farnum appeared in more Best Picture Oscar winning movies than anyone else. He was a character actor in 433 films including seven best picture winners – *The Life of Emile Zola* (1937), *Going My Way* (1944), *The Lost Weekend* (1945), *Gentleman's Agreement* (1947), *All About Eve* (1950), *The Greatest Show on Earth* (1952), and *Around the World in 80 Days* (1956).

810) Until the 19th century, the word hypocrites referred to actors.

811) The international distress signal one level less serious than Mayday is Pan-Pan; Securite is the third level.

812) Bees have five eyes.

813) "The Twist" by Chubby Checker is the only single by the same artist to go to number one twice in 1960 and 1961.

814) Eleven U.S. states are larger than the United Kingdom.

815) The Volkswagen Beetle was the first car model to sell 20 million units.

816) Canada issued the first Christmas stamp in 1898.

817) Killer whales aren't actually whales; they are dolphins. Their similarities with dolphins include teeth, streamlined bodies, rounded head, beak, echolocation, living in pods, and group hunting.

818) Dallas, Texas is named after George Mifflin Dallas who was U.S. vice president for James K. Polk in the 1840s.

819) The year 1 BC was followed by 1 AD.

820) If something is napiform, it is shaped like a turnip.

821) Washington has the only state flag that has an image of a president.

822) Michael Jackson wanted to buy Marvel Comics, so he could play Spider Man in his own movie.

823) Warren G. Harding had the largest feet, size 14, of any U.S. president.

824) "Expletive deleted" came into fashion as a result of the publication of the Watergate tapes transcript.

825) Wyoming has only two escalators in the entire state.

826) The first screen kiss between two men occurred in the 1927 movie *Wings*; it didn't cause any stir at the time.

827) The Vatican Bank has the only ATM in the world that allows users to perform transactions in Latin.

828) The first item bought and sold across the internet in 1971 was marijuana; Stanford students were buying from MIT students.

829) The Sargasso Sea is the only sea without a coastline (no land border). It is in the North Atlantic off the coast of the U.S. and is defined by currents.

830) The D-Day invasion password was Mickey Mouse.

831) Sylvester Stallone holds the record for the most years between Oscar nominations playing the same character; it was 39 years between *Rocky* in 1976 and *Creed* in 2015.

832) Jai-alai features the fastest moving ball of any sport with speeds up to 188 mph.

833) Mountain Dew was originally developed as a mixer for whiskey in the 1940s.

834) Maine is the only state that borders just one other state.

835) Of all countries that aren't landlocked, Monaco has the shortest coastline at 2.4 miles.

836) The earliest surviving written music dates to 1,400 BC, a hymn found in Syria.

837) A month beginning on a Sunday always has a Friday the 13th.

838) A poker hand with two black aces and two black eights is known as the "dead man's hand" because it is what Wild Bill Hickok was holding when he was killed.

839) A cockroach can live a week without its head. They are not dependent on their head or mouth to breath but will eventually die without it because they can't drink and die of thirst.

840) The world's smallest natural trees are dwarf willows which grow in Greenland and are only about two inches high.

841) The term blockbuster has meanings going back to large bombs in WWII, but as it is used to describe films, it was first used for *Jaws* in 1975.

842) Twelve people have walked on the Moon; but only three have been to the deepest part of the ocean. Director James Cameron is one of the three.

843) Patsy Cline was the first woman inducted into the Country Music Hall of Fame in 1973.

844) China has about half of all the pigs in the world.

845) The point in the ocean furthest from the nearest land is 1,670 miles from land; it is called Point Nemo and is in the South Pacific.

846) An elephant has 40,000 muscles in its trunk; there are about 640 muscles in the entire human body.

847) Mississippi was the last state to officially ratify the 13th amendment to the U.S. Constitution abolishing slavery in 2013. Mississippi ratified the amendment in 1995 but didn't notify the U.S. archivist and didn't officially complete the process until 2013.

848) The shellac resin used in varnish is a secretion of the lac insect.

849) In 1917, Germany invited Mexico to join WWI by attacking the U.S. to recover lost territories.

850) Hummingbirds have the biggest brain relative to their body size of any bird. Their brain is over 4% of their body weight.

851) St. Lucia is the only country in the world named after a woman; it is in the Caribbean and is named after St. Lucy of Syracuse from the 3rd century.

852) In Finland, the amount you are fined for a speeding ticket is based on your annual income; fines as high as 112,000 euros have been assessed for speeding with a multi-million-euro income.

853) Koalas are the sleepiest animal in the world; they sleep 22 hours per day.

854) Shark skin was once used commercially as sandpaper.

855) In the 18th century, a footman or valet was also sometimes called a fart catcher because they always walked behind their master or mistress.

856) Leonardo da Vinci was the first person to explain why the sky is blue.

857) Longtime NFL placekicker Fred Cox who played for the Minnesota Vikings from 1963-1977 invented the Nerf football.

858) Russian astronauts take guns into space to protect themselves from bears if they land off course.

859) In *The Bridge on the River Kwai*, the prisoners whistle the "Colonel Bogey March"; it was written in 1914 by a British army bandmaster.

860) George W. Bush is the only U.S. president who earned an MBA degree.

861) Female Greenland sharks reach sexual maturity at 150 years old. Greenland sharks grow to a similar size as great whites; they live in cold water and can live up to 400 years growing only 1 centimeter per year.

862) Woodrow Wilson is the only president with a PhD; he had a doctorate in history and political science.

863) The Los Angeles Dodgers MLB team got their name from the trolleys in Brooklyn, New York. The team was established in Brooklyn in 1883 and went through a number of different names before settling on the Trolley Dodgers which refers to the network of trolleys in Brooklyn which were a major cause of accidents at the time, so people were familiar with dodging trolleys. When the team moved to Los Angeles after the 1957 season, the shortened Dodgers name was kept.

864) Some snakes, Komodo dragons, sharks, and turkeys are all capable of virgin births.

865) Franklin D. Roosevelt was the first president to fly on official business; he made a secret trip to Casablanca in 1943.

866) The McMurdo Dry Valleys of Antarctica are the driest place on Earth; they are a row of snow free valleys that haven't seen water in millions of years.

867) Cuba has a maximum wage law regardless of job of $20 per month.

868) Only once in history has a submerged submarine deliberately sunk a submerged submarine. A British submarine sunk a German submarine in 1945.

869) A giraffe's tongue is black or purple to prevent sunburn since it is exposed a lot of the time while they eat.

870) French leader Charles de Gaulle had the nickname "The Great Asparagus"; he got the name in military school because of his looks.

871) Yellowstone National Park has most of the world's geysers.

872) Taumatawhakatangihangakoauauotamateaturipukakapikimaunga -horonukupokaiwhenuakitanatahu is the longest place name in the world; it is a hill in New Zealand.

873) Almost 100% of kangaroos are left-handed.

874) The word mortgage comes from a French word that means death contract.

875) Canada eats the most macaroni and cheese per capita.

876) At 59.9 degrees north latitude, St. Petersburg, Russia is the northernmost city in the world with a population over 1 million.

877) Including hunting dives, the peregrine falcon is the fastest bird in the world with speeds up to 242 mph.

878) Louis Bonaparte, Napoleon's brother, was called the "King of Rabbits" because he mispronounced the Dutch phrase "I am your King" and instead said "I am your rabbit" when he took over rule of the Netherlands in 1806.

879) According to legend, Attila the Hun died of a nosebleed on his wedding night.

880) There were 20 years between the first female in space and the first American female in space. Soviet Valentina Tereshkova was the first in 1963; Sally Ride was the first American in 1983.

881) In 1930, the movie *Ingagi* was marketed as a documentary of a 1926 expedition led by British explorers Sir Hubert Winstead and Captain Daniel Swayne who found a Congo tribe that worshipped a giant gorilla. It turned out to be a fake with Hollywood actors and Los Angeles children playing pygmies, but it was still the 11th highest grossing film of the 1930s.

882) The Russian October Revolution took place in November. It was October in the old Julian calendar but November in the current Gregorian calendar.

883) Chess has more books written about it than any other game.

884) With over 300,000 people, Murmansk, Russia is the most populous city north of the Arctic Circle.

885) The first automobile speeding ticket was issued in 1896 in England. The car was going 8 mph; the speed limit for cars was 2 mph. You could go over 2 mph if you had someone walk in front of the car waving a red flag to alert people.

886) Actor Sean Connery competed in the 1953 Mr. Universe bodybuilding competition.

887) Panama hats were originally made in Peru.

888) Albert Einstein was named *Time* magazine's Man of the Century in 1999.

889) During filming of *The Blues Brothers*, they had a special budget for cocaine during night shoots.

890) Of the 700 islands in the Bahamas, only 30 are inhabited.

891) The Fahrenheit and Celsius temperature scales are the same at 40 degrees below zero.

892) It takes a net worth of $770,000 to be in the top 1% of the world.

893) The Czech Republic drinks the most beer per person of any country with 235 liters per person annually.

894) When President Harry Truman visited Disneyland in 1957, he refused to go on the Dumbo ride because he didn't want to be seen riding in the symbol of the Republican party.

895) Humans and dogs are the only two animal species known to seek visual clues from another animal's eyes, and dogs only do it with humans.

896) Cal Hubbard was the first person inducted into the NFL and Major League Baseball Hall of Fame. He was an offensive lineman for New York and Green Bay in the 1920s and 1930s and was on four championship teams; he was also an MLB umpire.

897) Venus is often called the Earth's twin because it is nearly the same size and mass and has a similar composition.

898) In 1903, Thomas Edison electrocuted an elephant to prove the danger of alternating current. Edison was in a battle with Nikola Tesla over whether direct or alternating current would be implemented for the electric grid. Edison backed direct current, and he tried to prove the dangers of alternating current by going around the country electrocuting animals using alternating current. Alternating current still won out.

899) A newborn Bactrian camel doesn't have any humps. Baby camels don't get their humps until they start eating solid food.

900) Pierre, South Dakota is the only state capital that doesn't share any letters with its state.

Facts 901-1200

901) Australia made the world's first feature film in 1906.

902) The ancient Romans called early Christians atheists because they didn't worship pagan gods.

903) Episcopalian is the most common religious affiliation for U.S. presidents.

904) The Caspian Sea is the largest enclosed inland body of water in the world; it is considered a lake by some, but it has saltwater. It has 3.5 times more water than all the Great Lakes combined.

905) Lesotho is the only country that lies completely above 1,000 meters elevation; it is 11,720 square miles and is completely surrounded by South Africa.

906) The first Cannes Film Festival was called off after screening only one film because WWII broke out.

907) The national capital city of La Paz, Bolivia is one of the most fire safe cities in the world. At an elevation of 11,800 feet, it is difficult for fires to spread due to the low oxygen level.

908) In ancient China, only the aristocracy could have a Pekingese dog.

909) The word freelance comes from a knight who was free for hire.

910) Chinese astronauts are called taikonauts.

911) Sex therapist Dr. Ruth trained as a sniper in the Israeli army; they thought her short stature (4'7") would make her hard to see; she had an affinity for it.

912) "Mark twain" means two fathoms or twelve feet. It was used to call out the water depth on river boats; Samuel Clemens worked as a steamboat pilot and took his pen name from it.

913) Zimbabwe has the most official languages of any country with 16.

914) Alexander the Great, Julius Caesar, Genghis Khan, Napoleon, Mussolini, and Hitler all suffered from ailurophobia, a fear of cats.

915) Today's average American woman weighs as much as the average American man from the 1960s.

916) Jacqueline Kennedy Onassis edited Michael Jackson's autobiography *Moonwalk*.

917) According to suffragette Susan B. Anthony, the bicycle had "done more to emancipate women than anything else in the world."

918) A rhinoceros has three toes on each foot.

919) The first web site was launched by CERN in 1989.

920) Rock paper scissors originated in China about 2,000 years ago.

921) The United States is collectively overweight by about 4 billion pounds.

922) Napoleon was attacked by rabbits and had to retreat. In 1807, Napoleon had just signed the Treaty of Tilsit ending his war with Russia; to celebrate, he went on a rabbit hunt. Hundreds of rabbits had been gathered for the hunt in cages, but when they were released, they swarmed toward Napoleon and his men rather than running away. They swarmed Napoleon's legs and started climbing up him; he was forced to retreat to his coach and depart. Instead of wild rabbits, they had bought tame rabbits from farmers, so they weren't afraid of people and probably thought it was feeding time.

923) Only three people have died outside the Earth's atmosphere; they were aboard *Soyz 11* in 1971.

924) Pepsi was developed as a hangover remedy.

925) Walter Johnson has the highest season batting average ever for an MLB starting pitcher with .433 in 1925.

926) Horses have weak ciliary muscles which do a poor job of focusing their eyes, so they need to move their heads to adjust the focal length or angle of view until the image falls into view on a portion of their retina.

927) Ohio has the only non-rectangular state flag; it is a swallowtail shape.

928) Frank and Nancy Sinatra had the only number one song recorded by a father and daughter with "Something Stupid" in 1967.

929) Mead is the oldest alcoholic beverage to gain widespread popularity in about 2000 BC; it is made from honey.

930) For racing purposes, the birthday of all horses in the Northern Hemisphere is January 1. A horse born on December 31 is one year old on January 1.

931) Snickers is the world's best-selling candy bar.

932) There are 60 seconds in a minute and 360 degrees in a circle because the ancient Babylonians did math in base 60 instead of base 10 and developed the concepts.

933) Twenty-seven states are at least partly north of the southernmost point of Canada; Middle Island in Lake Erie is the most southern point of Canada. It is approximately the latitude of Chicago which means that Alaska, California, Connecticut, Idaho, Illinois, Indiana, Iowa, Maine, Massachusetts, Michigan, Minnesota, Montana, Nebraska, Nevada,

83

New Hampshire, New York, North Dakota, Ohio, Oregon, Pennsylvania, Rhode Island, South Dakota, Utah, Vermont, Washington, Wisconsin, and Wyoming are all at least partly north of Canada.

934) George Washington's salary as U.S. president was $25,000. Based on the change in the consumer price index, it would equate to over $700,000 in today's dollars; today's presidential salary is $400,000.

935) Sergio Leone originally wanted Henry Fonda to play the lead in *A Fistful of Dollars* but couldn't afford his salary. Many actors turned down the role before Clint Eastwood accepted and was paid $15,000 for the role.

936) The busiest muscles in the human body are in the eyes; it is estimated that they move 100,000 times a day.

937) Four is the only number spelled out in English that has the same number of letters as its value.

938) Sam Snead was the first PGA golfer to shoot their age in a tournament round; he shot a 67 at the 1979 Quad Cities Open.

939) The first U.S. television commercial ever broadcast was for Bulova watches in 1941.

940) Barry Manilow was Bette Midler's piano player before he went solo.

941) "American Pie" by Don McLean is the longest (minutes of play time) song to ever reach number one on the Billboard's Hot 100. It hit number one on January 15, 1972 and remained there for four weeks; the original version ran for 8 minutes and 38 seconds.

942) When it started, Starbucks only sold whole roasted coffee beans.

943) The 1920 Antwerp Olympics was the only Olympics where a single event was held in two different countries. The 12-foot dinghy sailing

event early races were held in Belgium, but the final two races were held in the Netherlands since the only two remaining competitors were Dutch.

944) Sweden has the largest permanent scale model of the solar system; the Sun is in Stockholm and represented by the largest hemispherical building in the world; the model is on a 1:20 million scale and stretches for 590 miles.

945) Maine is the only state with a one syllable name.

946) At up to 46 feet long, colossal squid are the largest invertebrate (no backbone) animal.

947) Napoleon wasn't short for his time. He was about 5 feet 7 inches; the average adult French male of his time was only 5 feet 5 inches, so he was taller than average. Some of the confusion is the units his height was reported in and that his personal guards who he was usually seen with were required to be quite tall.

948) Olivia de Haviland and Joan Fontaine are the only sisters to win acting Oscars.

949) Female ferrets can literally die if they don't mate. The female stays in heat until she mates; if she doesn't, very high levels of estrogen remain in her blood for a long time and can cause aplastic anemia and death. She doesn't have to get pregnant, but she must mate.

950) HBO put on a polka festival as its first attempt at original programming in 1973.

951) The most commonly used punctuation mark is the comma.

952) The opossum has the shortest known gestation period of any mammal at an average of just 12 days.

953) Water polo is the only sport where you can see teams defending goals of different sizes. The goal at the deep end is smaller than the goal at the shallow end. The inner sides of the goal posts are 10 feet apart; when the water depth is 5 feet or more, the crossbar is 3 feet from the water surface; when the water depth is less than 5 feet, the crossbar is 8 feet from the floor of the pool.

954) By volume, Tamu Massif is the world's largest volcano either active or extinct; it is 1,000 miles east of Japan under the Pacific Ocean and is extinct.

955) Only two golfers, Bobby Jones and Tiger Woods, have held all four major championships at the same time.

956) Marie Curie is the only person to win Nobel Prizes in two different areas of science – physics and chemistry.

957) About 50% of human DNA is the same as a banana.

958) Isaac Asimov is the only author to publish books in 9 of the 10 Dewey Decimal categories.

959) Oscar Hammerstein II is the only person named Oscar to win an Oscar.

960) The cornea is the only part of the human body without a blood supply.

961) The flag of the Philippines is flown with the blue side up in times of peace and with the red side up in times of war.

962) In ancient Greece, a normal jury had 500 people.

963) The Tibet region of China has the highest asphalt road in the world at 18,258 feet.

964) The world's largest gold depository is the Manhattan Federal Reserve Bank; it houses 7,700 tons of gold.

965) There are 88 constellations in the night sky.

966) Leo Fender, inventor of the Stratocaster and Telecaster guitars, couldn't play guitar.

967) Of all the senses, smell is most closely linked to memory.

968) La Paz, Bolivia at an elevation of 11,942 feet is the world's highest elevation national capital city.

969) Adolf Hitler described Switzerland as "a pimple on the face of Europe." He hated it and thought it had no right to exist; he had a planned invasion but never initiated it.

970) Alaska is the longest state from north to south at 1,479 miles.

971) Alaska has 6,640 miles of coastline which is more than the rest of the United States combined.

972) Only two elected U.S. vice presidents, Martin Van Buren and George H.W. Bush, were later elected president. Initially, the vice president was not specifically elected; they were the candidate who received the second most electoral votes.

973) Honolulu has the only royal palace in the U.S.

974) The term sniper originates from how hard it is to shoot the snipe bird.

975) *Lawrence of Arabia* is the only Best Picture Oscar winner without any female speaking roles.

976) The giant and colossal squid have the largest eye of any animal at up to 11 inches in diameter.

977) The worldwide life expectancy at birth is 69 years.

978) A group of unicorns is called a blessing.

979) The highest blood alcohol level ever recorded that didn't result in death was 0.91% which is more than twice the normal lethal level. The typical level for legally drunk is 0.08%.

980) Alfred Carlton Gilbert, a 1908 Olympic gold medal pole vaulter, invented the Erector Set toy.

981) It only takes 23 people in a group to have a 50% chance that two will have the same birthday. This is known as the Birthday Paradox; the probability goes up to 99.9% with just 70 people.

982) In 1935, Jesse Owens set world records in three different events in 45 minutes. At a Big Ten track and field meet, he set world records in the long jump, 220-yard sprint, and 220-yard low hurdles and tied the world record for the 100-yard dash.

983) If uncoiled, the DNA in all cells of the human body would stretch about 10 billion miles.

984) Eight presidents were born as British subjects – Washington, John Adams, Jefferson, Madison, Monroe, John Quincy Adams, Jackson, William Henry Harrison.

985) The ZIP in ZIP Code stands for Zone Improvement Plan.

986) Canada's Wasaga Beach on the shores of Lake Huron is the world's longest freshwater beach; it is 14 miles long.

987) The harmonica is the world's best-selling musical instrument.

988) Barack Obama was the first sitting U.S. president to visit Hiroshima.

989) Arkansas has the only active diamond mine in the U.S.

990) Based on active enrollment, Indira Gandhi National Open University is the largest university in the world. It is a distance learning university in New Delhi, India and has over 4 million students.

991) Hexakosioihexekontahexaphobia is the fear of the number 666.

992) Petrichor is the word for the pleasant odor after a rain. Streptomyces bacteria in the soil produce a molecule called geosmin which is released into the air when rain hits the ground producing the smell. Humans are extremely sensitive to the smell.

993) Australia has the lowest average elevation of any continent at 1,080 feet.

994) The average adult human heart pumps about 2,000 gallons of blood each day.

995) Your hearing is less sharp after you eat too much.

996) The Eskimo kiss of rubbing noses isn't really a kiss; it is called a kunik and is typically used as an expression of affection between an adult and a child. The Inuit kiss on the lips like many other cultures.

997) In the 19th century, doctors treated hysteria in women by inducing orgasms; the vibrator was invented as a result of this practice.

998) A group of owls is called a parliament.

999) *Pocahontas* was the first Disney animated film based on the life of a real person.

1000) Lionel and Ethel Barrymore are the only brother and sister to win acting Oscars.

1001) Of the 25 highest peaks in the world, 10 are in the Himalayas.

1002) The story of Cinderella originated in China.

1003) The first patented work uniform in the U.S. was the Playboy Bunny outfit.

1004) By volume, Lake Baikal in Russia is the largest freshwater lake in the world. It has a maximum depth of 5,387 feet and contains about 20% of the total unfrozen surface freshwater in the world.

1005) The letter x begins the fewest words in the English language.

1006) Truth or Consequences, New Mexico was named for a radio game show; the game show offered to broadcast from the first town that renamed itself after the show. Hot Springs, New Mexico won the honor and renamed itself in 1950.

1007) The world's most widely used vegetable is the onion.

1008) Pirates wore earrings to improve their eyesight; they believed the precious metals in an earring had healing powers.

1009) Rhinotillexomania is excessive nose picking.

1010) About 24,000 people are killed worldwide by lightning each year.

1011) The Statue of Liberty gets hit by lightning about 600 times per year.

1012) The first published use of the word hello was in 1827; hello is a relatively recent word and was initially used to attract attention or express surprise; it didn't get its current meaning until the telephone arrived.

1013) The sport of cricket originated the term home run.

1014) The International Space Station is the most expensive man-made object ever built at a cost of $160 billion.

1015) In the movie *The China Syndrome*, the title refers to a hypothetical catastrophic failure where a nuclear reactor melts through the floor of its containment system and penetrates the earth's surface as if traveling through toward China.

1016) Kim is the most common surname for an Olympic athlete.

1017) Orson Welles was only 25 years old when he co-wrote, produced, directed and starred in *Citizen Kane* which is still widely regarded as the greatest movie ever made.

1018) Einstein had to give his Nobel Prize money to his ex-wife as part of their divorce settlement.

1019) The first internet domain name was registered in 1985

1020) Bob Mathias of the United States is the youngest male track and field Olympic gold medalist ever; he was 17 years old when he won the 1948 decathlon.

1021) Three countries are completely surrounded by one other country; they are Lesotho (surrounded by South Africa), and Vatican City and San Marino (both surrounded by Italy).

1022) Queen Victoria was prescribed marijuana for her menstrual cramps.

1023) Metallica is the first and only music group to play on all seven continents.

1024) George Reeves, television's original Superman, was one of Scarlett's beaus, Brent Tarleton, in *Gone with the Wind*.

1025) The longest English word with one syllable has nine letters; there are several words – scratched, screeched, stretched, straights, strengths, etc.

1026) The only land mammal native to New Zealand is the bat.

1027) Abraham Lincoln was the first president born outside the original 13 states.

1028) The first NFL indoor game took place in 1932. With 30 below zero temperatures in Chicago, the Bears played a game indoors against the Portsmouth Spartans in the Chicago Stadium which was used mainly for horse shows; they played on a modified 80-yard field.

1029) In the opening credits for the first season of *Gilligan's Island*, the U.S. flag is at half-mast as the *Minnow* pulls out of harbor because of John F. Kennedy's assassination. The scene was filmed in November 1963 in Hawaii; the cast and crew learned of Kennedy's assassination on the last day of filming.

1030) Roger Maris still holds the American League record for most home runs in a season from 1961; the seasons that have surpassed his record have all been in the National League.

1031) The youngest Olympic medalist ever in an individual event was 12 years old in the 200-meter women's breaststroke swimming in 1936.

1032) By volume, the world's largest pyramid is in Mexico; the Great Pyramid of Cholula has a base of 450 meters each side and a height of 66 meters.

1033) There are about 6,900 living languages in the world. Just 6% of the languages account for 94% of the world's population. About half of the languages have fewer than 10,000 speakers, and one-quarter have fewer than 1,000 speakers.

1034) Mercury and Venus are the only two planets in our solar system that don't have moons.

1035) Enrico Caruso had the first record to sell over a million copies in 1902.

1036) In polo, you are you banned from playing left-handed. If a left-handed and right-handed player went for the ball, they would collide.

1037) There are six dots in each letter in the Braille system.

1038) Five presidents regularly wore beards while in office - Lincoln, Grant, Hayes, Garfield, Benjamin Harrison.

1039) Alaska is both the westernmost and easternmost state; parts of Alaska stretch into the Eastern Hemisphere.

1040) St. Lucia is the smallest population country with two or more Nobel Prize winners; it is in the Caribbean with 185,000 people and two Nobel Prize winners.

1041) Alligators are only naturally found in the United States and China.

1042) Stevie Wonder is the youngest solo artist to have a number one hit on Billboard's Hot 100 at age 13 with "Fingertips Part 2" in 1963.

1043) By area, Great Salt Lake is the largest lake entirely within one state.

1044) Inspired by burrs, George de Mestral invented Velcro in the 1940s.

1045) Mars is red because it is covered in iron oxide (rust).

1046) Minnie Mouse's full first name is Minerva.

1047) Since the start of the Winter Olympics, five athletes have won medals at both the winter and summer games. They are Eddie Eagan (U.S.), Jacob Tullin Thams (Norway), Christa Luding-Rothenburger (East Germany), Clara Hughes (Canada), and Lauryn Williams (U.S.).

1048) Checkers originated in Egypt as early as 200 BC.

1049) The most perfectly round natural object known to man in the universe is a star 5,000 light-years away; prior to this discovery, the Sun was the most perfectly round known natural object.

1050) Scatomancy was popular in ancient Egypt; it is telling the future through someone's poop.

1051) A group of rhinoceros is called a crash.

1052) English is the official language of the most countries.

1053) Today's British accent first appeared among the British upper class about the time of the American Revolution. Before that, the British accent was like Americans.

1054) Marilyn Monroe was the first *Playboy* centerfold.

1055) Hawaii has the most rainfall of any state with 63.7 inches mean annual precipitation.

1056) The video game company Nintendo was founded in 1889; it originally produced handmade playing cards.

1057) The wheel was invented about 3500 BC.

1058) Early in his career, Picasso was so poor he burned most of his early work to keep his apartment warm.

1059) The most searched tutorial on YouTube is how to kiss.

1060) Canada eats the most donuts per capita; the presence of 3,000 Tim Hortons restaurants is a major factor.

1061) Satan is the Hebrew word for adversary.

1062) Frances Folsom Cleveland is the youngest U.S. first lady ever. She was 21 when she married Grover Cleveland in the White House; he was 49.

1063) The first accurate eyewitness report of the Wright brothers' first flight appeared in the magazine *Gleanings in Bee Culture*.

1064) Teeth are the only part of the human body that cannot repair itself.

1065) The Northern Hemisphere is warmer than the Southern Hemisphere by 1.5 degrees Celsius; it is due to ocean circulation.

1066) The button on the top of a baseball cap is called a squatchee.

1067) Spencer Tracy and Tom Hanks are the only two actors who have won consecutive Best Actor Oscars. Spencer Tracy won for *Captains Courageous* (1937) and *Boys Town* (1938), and Tom Hanks won for *Philadelphia* (1993) and *Forrest Gump* (1994).

1068) *The Howdy Doody Show* (1947-1960) was the first U.S. television show to broadcast 1,000 episodes.

1069) At 37.8 degrees south latitude, Melbourne, Australia is the southernmost city in the world with a population over 1 million.

1070) When the Persians were at war with the Egyptians, they rounded up and released as many cats as they could on the battlefield. Knowing the Egyptians reverence for cats, they knew they would not want to do anything to hurt the cats; the Persians won the battle.

1071) Zero can't be represented in Roman numerals.

1072) No witches were burned at the stake during the Salem witch trials; 20 were executed, but most were hung, and none were burned.

1073) New Mexico has the lowest percent of its area that is water of any state at 0.2%.

1074) About 100 billion people have died in all of human history.

1075) Bears have the best sense of smell of any land animal. Black bears have been observed to travel 18 miles in a straight line to a food source; grizzlies can find an elk carcass underwater, and polar bears can smell a seal through three feet of ice.

1076) In 1997, Pope John Paul II decided that Saint Isidore of Seville would be the patron saint of the internet.

1077) According to his wife, Abraham Lincoln's hobby was cats. He loved them and could play with them for hours; he once allowed a cat to eat from the table at a formal White House dinner.

1078) The most used letter in the English alphabet is e.

1079) Dogs were the first domesticated animal up to 40,000 years ago.

1080) In 1958, Robert Heft designed the current 50-star U.S. flag as a part of a junior high history class project.

1081) In 1889, Germany was the first country to introduce old age pensions.

1082) Caviar was served free in old west saloons to make customers drink more.

1083) James is the most common first name of U.S. presidents with six presidents - Madison, Monroe, Polk, Buchanan, Garfield, Carter.

1084) Polo is played on the largest field of any sport; the field is 300 yards by 160 yards.

1085) French mime Marcel Marceau spoke the only word in Mel Brooks' 1976 film *Silent Movie.*

1086) A domestic cat shares 95.6% of its DNA with a tiger.

1087) Gerald Ford is the only U.S. president to not have been elected president or vice president.

1088) The tongue is the fastest healing part of the human body.

1089) The word stymie originated in golf. Until 1952 when the rules were changed, balls had to remain in place, so you could be stymied by having another player's ball between your ball and the hole; you had to loft your ball over the other ball.

1090) Equestrian and sailing are the only Olympic sports where men and women compete head to head.

1091) A baby blue whale gains about 200 pounds of weight each day.

1092) The first published crossword puzzle was in the *New York World* newspaper on December 21, 1913.

1093) Roman gladiator fights started as a part of funerals; when wealthy nobles died, they would have bouts at the graveside.

1094) Iceland has the highest per capita electricity consumption; it is about four times higher than the U.S.

1095) Leprosy is probably the oldest known infectious disease in humans. Its roots may stretch back millions of years.

1096) The pound or number symbol (#) is also called an octothorpe; the name is believed to have been made up by workers at Bell Telephone Labs who needed a name for the symbol on the telephone keypad.

1097) Grover Cleveland was the only president to get married at the White House.

1098) Aluminum is the most abundant metal in the Earth's crust.

1099) James Bond creator Ian Fleming wrote the book *Chitty-Chitty-Bang-Bang: The Magical Car* upon which the movie was based.

1100) Ulysses S. Grant was the first president to run against a woman candidate; Virginia Woodhull was a nominee of the Equal Rights Party in 1872.

1101) The remains of England's King Richard III were found buried under a parking lot in Leicester England in 2013; he was the last English king to die on the battlefield in 1485.

1102) Warren Moon is the first player ever in both the Pro Football Hall of Fame and the Canadian Football Hall of Fame.

1103) Ted Kaczynski was called the Unabomber because his early targets were universities (un) and airlines (a).

1104) President Barack Obama collected Spiderman and Conan the Barbarian comic books.

1105) All the bacteria in an average human body collectively weigh about four pounds.

1106) According to the Bible, Goliath was six cubits tall or about nine feet.

1107) On average, men say 12,500 words per day; women say 22,000.

1108) William Shakespeare was the first person other than royalty to appear on a British stamp.

1109) Fireflies are a species of beetle.

1110) The ancient Romans used human urine as mouthwash; it was supposed to purge bacteria, and physicians claimed it whitened teeth and made them stronger. Upper class women paid for bottled Portuguese urine since it was supposed to be the strongest on the continent.

1111) The most common symbol on flags of the world is a star.

1112) *Saturday Night Live* was the first U.S. network television show to use the "F" word.

1113) Hippopotomonstrosesquippedaliophobia is the fear of long words.

1114) The Great Pyramid at Giza was the world's tallest man-made structure for over 3,800 years.

1115) Sweden's official Twitter account is managed by a random citizen who is chosen each week.

1116) Indonesia has on average the shortest people in the world with an average of 5'2" for men and 4'10" for women.

1117) An orchestra usually tunes up to the oboe; its sound is easy to hear, and its pitch is more stable than strings.

1118) At 238 minutes, *Gone with the Wind* is the longest movie to ever win the Best Picture Oscar.

1119) A Danish journalist covering the 1900 Paris Olympics won a gold medal. He was recruited to replace an ill team member on the combined Sweden/Denmark tug of war team, and they went on to win gold.

1120) Apollo astronauts trained in Iceland because they felt it most resembled the surface of the moon.

1121) Windsor Castle is the largest inhabited castle in the world at 590,000 square feet.

1122) The original Peeping Tom was looking at Lady Godiva.

1123) Gymnast Cathy Rigby was the first woman to pose nude for *Sports Illustrated.*

1124) In 1917, Janette Rankin from Montana become the first woman elected to the U.S. Congress.

1125) Nikita Khrushchev gave Caroline Kennedy her dog Pushinka while her dad was president.

1126) The Aztecs played a game called ollamalitzli which was like basketball. They had to get a hard rubber ball through a stone hoop.

1127) Lake Maracaibo, Venezuela has the most lightning strikes of any place in the world. Lightning storms occur for about 10 hours a night, 140 to 160 nights a year, for a total of about 1.2 million lightning discharges per year.

1128) The first person in space who wasn't American or Russian was Czech, Vladimir Remek in 1978.

1129) The material that became Kleenex was originally used for gas mask filters in WWI.

1130) Oscar Zoroaster Phadrig Isaac Norman Henkle Emmannuel Ambroise Diggs is the real name of The Wizard of Oz.

1131) In ancient Rome, women drank turpentine to make their urine smell sweet like roses.

1132) The CIA spent $20 million in the 1960s training cats to spy on the Soviet Union; it didn't work.

1133) In the song "Yankee Doodle", the term macaroni means stylish or fashionable. In late 18th century England, the term macaroni came to mean stylish or fashionable; in the song, it is used to mock the Americans who think they can be stylish by simply sticking a feather in their cap.

1134) Fifteen people have won all four major American entertainment awards (Oscar, Emmy, Tony, Grammy). They are Richard Rogers, Helen Hayes, Rita Moreno, John Gielgud, Audrey Hepburn, Marvin Hamlisch, Mel Brooks, Whoopi Goldberg, Jonathan Tunick, Mike Nichols, Scott Rudin, Robert Lopez, John Legend, Tim Rice, and Andrew Lloyd Weber.

1135) The NFL Green Bay Packers get their name from the Indian Packing Company. The team founder Curly Lambeau asked his employer for equipment, and his employer agreed to sponsor the team if he named them the Packers.

1136) The mangrove is the only tree that grows in saltwater.

1137) Istanbul, Turkey is the only major city in the world located on two continents, Europe and Asia.

1138) Christ's name translated directly from Hebrew to English would be Joshua; Jesus comes about by translating Hebrew to Greek to Latin to English.

1139) Taking cocaine increases the chance of having a heart attack within the hour by 2400%.

1140) Between 1530 and 1780, over 1 million Europeans were captured and sold as slaves to North Africa.

1141) Fraser Clarke Heston, Charlton Heston's real son, played the infant Moses in *The Ten Commandments*.

1142) In average lawn or garden soil, a mole can dig 12-15 feet per hour.

1143) The word plagiarism comes from the Latin word plagiarius which means kidnapper.

1144) The famous Hollywood sign in Los Angeles originally said Hollywoodland. The sign was erected in 1923 as an advertisement for an upscale real estate development called Hollywoodland; it was changed to its current form in 1949.

1145) Detroit is the only U.S. city to win three of the four major professional sports championships in the same year; in 1935, it won the NFL, NBA, and NHL championships.

1146) Beetles are the most common group of insects. Flies are the second most common, and bees and ants are third.

1147) *The Cisco Kid* (1950-1956) was the first television series filmed in color. It was filmed in color from its first season, but its broadcasts were still black and white at the time.

1148) Theodore Roosevelt banned Christmas trees from the White House because he had environmental concerns.

1149) Neil Armstrong didn't say "one small step for man" when he set foot on the Moon. He said, "one small step for a man"; that is what Armstrong claims he said, and audio analysis confirms it. It has been misquoted all these years.

1150) Leonardo da Vinci first proposed the concept of contact lenses.

1151) Cleopatra was Greek.

1152) Supermodel Cindy Crawford was valedictorian of her high school class and had a scholarship to study chemical engineering at Northwestern University. She dropped out after one semester to pursue modeling full time.

1153) Extant is the opposite of extinct.

1154) Play-Doh was originally created as a wallpaper cleaning putty to remove coal dust in the 1930s.

1155) Tsutomu Yamaguchi is the only recognized person in the world to survive both the Hiroshima and Nagasaki atomic bomb blasts. He was in Hiroshima on business for the first bomb and then returned home to Nagasaki.

1156) Cappuccino gets its name from the similarity of its color to the robes of the Capuchin monks.

1157) A mouse's sperm is bigger than an elephant's sperm. Large animals tend to have high numbers of smaller sperm.

1158) Walt Disney was head of the committee that organized the opening day ceremonies for the 1960 Squaw Valley, California Winter Olympics.

1159) King Zog of Albania who was coronated in 1928 was Europe's only Muslim king.

1160) Walmart is the largest seller of firearms in the United States.

1161) Vito Corleone is the only movie character that has won Oscars for two different actors; Marlon Brando won for *The Godfather,* and Robert de Niro won for *The Godfather Part II.*

1162) Relative to its own weight, the strongest organism known is the gonorrhea bacterium. They can pull with a force of 100,000 times their body weight which is comparable to a 150-pound person pulling 7,500 tons.

1163) Abraham Lincoln imposed the first U.S. federal income tax.

1164) Most of the world's supply of cork comes from cork oak trees predominantly in Portugal and Spain.

1165) A human sneeze travels about 100 mph.

1166) In the 1932 Los Angeles Olympic games, the men's steeplechase finalists ran an extra 364 yards because the race official lost track of the laps, and the entire field ran an extra lap.

1167) Birds don't urinate. They convert excess nitrogen to uric acid instead of urea; it is less toxic and doesn't need to be diluted as much. It goes out with their other waste and saves water, so they don't have to drink as much.

1168) At the first modern Olympics, silver medals were awarded to the winners; second place received bronze medals.

1169) In Germany, you can't name your child Matti because it doesn't indicate gender; Germany has laws regarding the naming of children including that the name must indicate gender and must not negatively affect the child's well-being.

1170) President Grover Cleveland twice served as an executioner in his duty as a sheriff.

1171) Bingo is the name of the dog on the Cracker Jack box.

1172) American poet Emma Lazarus wrote the words that are engraved on the Statue of Liberty in 1883 to raise money for the statue's pedestal.

1173) The Maillard reaction is the process where food browns during cooking.

1174) Montpelier, Vermont is the only state capital without a McDonald's.

1175) A polar bear's fur isn't white. It is transparent and appears white only because it reflects visible light.

1176) In 1932, Mildred "Babe" Didrikson Zaharias won the team championship single-handedly at the AAU national track and field meet. She competed in 8 out of 10 events; she won five and tied for first in a sixth event. She won the team championship despite being the only member of her team.

1177) The oceans are 71% of the Earth's surface but only account for 0.02% of the Earth's mass.

1178) Owls have three eyelids – one for blinking, one for sleeping, and one for keeping their eyes clean.

1179) At one point in the year, it is the same local time for people living in Oregon and Florida. A small part of eastern Oregon is in the mountain time zone, and a small part of western Florida is in the central time zone. When the change from daylight saving time to standard time is made; these two areas share the same time for one hour after the central time zone has fallen back to standard time and before the mountain time zone has.

1180) The 2016 Rio de Janeiro Olympics was the first Summer Olympics to be held entirely during the winter. The other two Summer Olympics in the Southern Hemisphere had taken place at least partly in the spring.

1181) Mongolia is the least densely populated country in the world; areas like Greenland have even lower density but aren't independent countries.

1182) Antarctica is the windiest continent.

1183) During the 1980s, Pablo Escobar's drug cartel was spending $2,500 per month on rubber bands to hold all the cash.

1184) *Gone with the Wind* has sold more tickets than any other movie in the U.S. About 208 million tickets have been sold; the U.S. population in 1939 when it was released was 131 million.

1185) Alabama's state constitution is longest constitution in the world at 310,000 words.

1186) A catfish is the only animal that naturally has an odd number of whiskers.

1187) Instead of 212 degrees Fahrenheit, the boiling point of water at the top of Mount Everest is about 160 degrees.

1188) The arrector pili muscles, located near the root of human hair follicles, are responsible for goosebumps.

1189) The mouthwash Listerine was originally created as a surgical disinfectant.

1190) Up until 1954, traffic stop signs in the U.S. were yellow.

1191) George Bernard Shaw and Bob Dylan are the only two people to win both a Nobel Prize and an Oscar. George Bernard Shaw won the Nobel Literature Prize in 1925 and the Best Adapted Screenplay Oscar for *Pygmalion* in 1936; Bob Dylan won the Best Original Song Oscar for "Things Have Changed" from *Wonder Boys* in 2000 and the Nobel Literature Prize in 2016.

1192) According to the Old Testament, Noah planted the first vineyard.

1193) Over the last two centuries, each year has added about three months to average human life expectancy.

1194) Vitali Klitschko is the first world boxing champion to hold a PhD degree. He was a three-time world heavyweight champion starting in 1999 and ending in 2013 and got his PhD in sports science in 2000. He has also served as mayor of Kiev and in the Ukrainian parliament.

1195) Ronald Reagan's pet name for Nancy was mommy poo pants.

1196) *60 Minutes* was the first U.S. network television show without a theme song.

1197) Southern Florida is the only place in the world that alligators and crocodiles exist together naturally in the wild.

1198) James Buchanan was the only U.S. president that was never married. Historians speculate that he may have been the first gay president. He developed a very close relationship with William Rufus King, an Alabama senator who was Franklin Pierce's Vice President. Buchanan and King lived together and were openly close with each other, causing people to refer to King as Buchanan's better half.

1199) *I Love Lucy* is generally credited with inventing the television rerun. During Lucille Ball's pregnancy, they had to rerun episodes.

1200) Psychologist William Marston was one of the inventors of the polygraph and created the comics character Wonder Woman and her Lasso of Truth.

Facts 1201-1500

1201) President Thomas Jefferson is commonly credited with inventing the swivel chair.

1202) If the earth's history was condensed to 24 hours, humans would appear at 11:58:43 pm.

1203) A crocodile can't stick its tongue out. It is attached to the roof of their mouth; their tongue helps keep their throat closed underwater so they can open their mouth to hunt prey.

1204) *Meet the Press* is the longest running television show of any kind in the U.S.; it started in 1947 and is still running.

1205) Edgar Allan Poe created mystery fiction's first detective in 1841's *The Murders in the Rue Morgue.*

1206) Before 1687, clocks didn't have minute hands.

1207) Florida is the only state on the east coast to fall partly in the central time zone.

1208) Tuna need to swim continuously to breathe. They can't pump water through their gills without swimming.

1209) A pirate who is yelling "Avast, ye mateys" is telling his mates to stop or cease.

1210) Pocahontas is buried along the Thames River in England; she died during a visit to England.

1211) Fruit flies were the very first animal to go into space. In 1947, they went up in a captured German V2 rocket; they were recovered alive.

1212) Caffeine is lethal in high enough doses; it would take about 70 cups of coffee to kill a 150-pound person.

1213) A hippopotamus' skin is two inches thick; it is difficult even for bullets to penetrate it.

1214) Cerebral hypoxia is the end cause of every human death. Lack of oxygen to the brain is the final cause of death regardless what initiates it.

1215) A group of flamingos is called a flamboyance.

1216) Sudan has the more pyramids than any other country; it has almost twice as many as Egypt.

1217) The Faroe Islands have the most Nobel Prize winners per capita. With 50,000 people located halfway between Norway and Iceland, they have one Nobel Prize winner.

1218) Thomas Jefferson had the largest personal book collection in the U.S. and sold it to become part of the Library of Congress after the library was destroyed in the War of 1812.

1219) Philosopher Plato was a double winner at the ancient Olympics. He won in plankration which was a submission sport combining elements of wrestling and boxing but with very few rules; only eye gouging and biting were banned.

1220) The logo of the Royal Air Force of New Zealand is the kiwi, a flightless bird.

1221) In Germany, there is no punishment for a prisoner who tries to escape if no other laws are broken. They assume the desire for freedom is natural.

1222) Orville Wright was the pilot in the first fatal airplane crash.

1223) The United States doesn't have an official language.

1224) The largest named bottle of wine is Melchizedek; it has a volume of 30 liters, equivalent to 40 standard 750 ml wine bottles.

1225) In 1893, Grover Cleveland was the first president to have a child born in the White House.

1226) Juliet is 13 years old in Shakespeare's *Romeo and Juliet.*

1227) Canada has more lakes than the rest of the world combined; it has more than 2 million lakes.

1228) The first television was installed at the British Prime Minister's residence at 10 Downing Street, London in 1930. Prime Minister Ramsay MacDonald and his family watched the first television drama ever on it.

1229) The Bible doesn't say how many wise men there were. It says wise men and mentions the gifts; there is no indication of how many wise men.

1230) London didn't get back to its pre-WWII population until 2015.

1231) Denmark's flag has lasted longer without change than any other country; is has been the same since at least 1370.

1232) At 64 degrees north latitude, Reykjavik, Iceland is the world's most northerly national capital city.

1233) Of the 48 contiguous states, Olympia, Washington is the most northern state capital.

1234) The mental disorder sluggish schizophrenia was diagnosed up to the 1970s as a made-up disorder that the Soviet Union used to confine dissenters. It was supposedly a very slow developing schizophrenia, so they could use the diagnosis on anyone.

1235) Sea otters hold hands while they are sleeping, so they don't drift apart.

1236) Washington is the most commonly occurring place name in the U.S.

1237) China is the largest country with only one time zone; geographically, it has five time zones, but it chooses to use one standard time.

1238) Twenty-two countries don't maintain an army including Andorra, Costa Rica, Panama, Grenada, Haiti, Iceland, and Liechtenstein.

1239) In the movie *Jaws*, Quint describes the sinking of a ship during WWII and how the sharks attacked the survivors. His story is based on the real story of the *USS Indianapolis*. After four days in the water, only 317 of the original 1,196-man crew were rescued. Estimates of how many died due to shark attacks range from a few dozen to 150; it is the U.S. Navy's single worst loss at sea and the worst shark attack in recorded history.

1240) Antarctica has the highest average elevation of any continent with an average of 8,200 feet.

1241) The singular of graffiti is graffito.

1242) Jimmy Carter was the first president born in a hospital.

1243) *Gone with the Wind* had the first posthumous Oscar ever awarded for screenwriter Sidney Howard.

1244) On average, cats sleep 15 hours per day.

1245) The oldest Summer Olympics medalist was 72; he medaled in shooting in 1920.

1246) Nescafe was the first instant coffee in 1938.

1247) *Snow White and the Seven Dwarfs* (1937) was the first full length color cartoon talking picture.

1248) Cleopatra married two of her brothers.

1249) A Canadian equestrian rider competed in every Olympics from 1972 to 2012 except the boycotted 1980 games. He had one silver medal in 2008 and holds the record for most Olympic games anyone has ever competed in at 10.

1250) Antarctica is the driest continent; it only gets about eight inches of precipitation annually and is considered a desert.

1251) On taking power in 1959, Fidel Castro banned the board game Monopoly and ordered all sets destroyed; he viewed it as the embodiment of capitalism.

1252) If you drilled a hole straight through the center of the Earth to the other side and jumped in, it would take 42 minutes to get to the other side. You would accelerate until you got to the center and then decelerate until you got to the other side where your speed would be zero again.

1253) Kathryn Bigelow was the first female Best Director Oscar winner for *The Hurt Locker* (2008).

1254) The Russian team arrived 12 days late for the 1908 London Olympics because Russia was still using the old Julian calendar instead of the Gregorian calendar.

1255) Facebook is cited in one-third of American divorce filings.

1256) Louisa Adams and Melania Trump are the only two U.S. first ladies born outside the U.S.

1257) The first vending machine in the United States in 1888 dispensed Tutti-Frutti gum.

1258) The world's first underwater tunnel was under the Thames River in London in 1843.

1259) The airport in Genoa, Italy limits liquids to three ounces but makes an exception for pesto sauce which is a Genoa specialty. They have a special pesto scanner.

1260) Oregon has the only two-sided (different designs on each side) state flag.

1261) In golf, a score of four under par on a single hole is called a condor. There have only been four verified; all were hole in ones on par five holes.

1262) Producer Julia Phillips was the first woman to win a Best Picture Oscar for *The Sting* (1973).

1263) Switzerland last went to war with another country in 1515.

1264) On average, the Antarctic ice sheet is one mile thick.

1265) The giraffe has the longest tail of any land animal; their tail can be up to eight feet long.

1266) *The Comedy of Errors* is the only Shakespeare play that mentions America.

1267) Big Bird on *Sesame Street* is 8 feet 2 inches tall.

1268) Peter Sellers, Alan Arkin, Roger Moore, Roberto Benigni, and Steve Martin have all played Inspector Clouseau in *Pink Panther* movies.

1269) The Sun has made about 20 orbits around the center of the Milky Way Galaxy in its life.

1270) Due to its unique chemical qualities, honey can remain edible for centuries; 3,000-year-old edible honey has been found in tombs.

1271) An aircraft's black box flight recorder is orange.

1272) *Ben-Hur*, *Titanic*, and *The Lord of the Rings: The Return of the King* are tied for the most Oscars at 11 each.

1273) *Midnight Cowboy* is the only X-rated movie to win the Best Picture Oscar. It was X-rated at the time of the award; in 1971, its rating was changed to R.

1274) Juneau Alaska is the least accessible state capital; you have to fly or take a boat.

1275) Babe Ruth wore a cabbage leaf under his cap; he put chilled cabbage leaves under his cap to keep cool.

1276) Yuma, Arizona is the sunniest city in the world; it averages 4,015 hours of sunshine annually or about 90% of daylight hours.

1277) Roman gladiator bouts only resulted in death about 10 to 20% of the time. The bouts were generally not intended to be to the death; gladiators were expensive, and promoters didn't want to see them die needlessly.

1278) In Greek mythology, they believed redheads turned into vampires when they died.

1279) A Shabbat elevator is one that works in a special mode and stops at every floor to avoid pushing buttons which is considered doing work on the Sabbath.

1280) In your lifetime, your long-term memory can hold about 1 quadrillion bits of information.

1281) Flamingos can only eat when their head is upside down.

1282) Eighty percent of the world's lawyers live in the United States.

1283) At the time he retired, Wayne Gretzky held 61 NHL records.

1284) The Coast Guard was the first U.S. military academy to admit women in 1976.

1285) The greyhound is the only dog breed specifically mentioned in the Bible.

1286) Orlando, Florida is the most visited U.S. city; New York City is second.

1287) Limpet teeth are the strongest natural material known to man. Limpets are small snail like creatures; a single spaghetti strand of their teeth material could hold 3,300 pounds.

1288) Marguerite Norris was the first woman to have her name engraved on the Stanley Cup. In 1952, she became the first female chief executive in NHL history after inheriting the Detroit Red Wings presidency from her father James Norris Sr. on his death. In 1954, the Red Wings defeated the Montreal Canadiens in the finals making her the first woman to have her name engraved on the Stanley Cup.

1289) Time, person, and year are the three most commonly used nouns in English.

1290) Eight presidents have been left-handed: Garfield, Hoover, Truman, Ford, Reagan, G.W. Bush, Clinton, Obama.

1291) Eigengrau is the name for the dark gray color the eyes see in perfect darkness as a result of optic nerve signals.

1292) Charles Addams' *New Yorker* cartoons of a spooky husband and wife were the inspiration for *The Addams Family* and Boris Badenov and Natasha Fatale of *Rocky and Bullwinkle and Friends.*

1293) Dragonflies may have the best vision of any animal. Humans have three light sensitive proteins in the eye for red, blue, and green (tri-chromatic vision); dragonflies have up to 33. Their bulbous eyes have 30,000 facets and can see in all directions at once.

1294) The brain is the highest percentage fat human organ. It is up to 60% fat, so everyone is a fathead.

1295) *The Lord of the Rings: The Return of the King* has the highest number of on-screen deaths of any movie with 836.

1296) Composer Vivaldi was also a priest.

1297) In 1990, Benazir Bhutto of Pakistan was the first elected head of a nation to give birth in office.

1298) The blood red sky in Edvard Munch's famous painting *The Scream* is believed to be due to the Krakatoa volcanic eruption in 1883 rather than the artist's imagination. The dust from the eruption created a red sky in Norway that Munch witnessed.

1299) Between 1838 and 1960, most of all photos taken were of babies.

1300) Only one time in NHL history has a goalie been credited with scoring a goal against an opposing goalie (not an empty net goal). On March 21, 2013 during a game between the New Jersey Devils and Carolina Hurricanes, a delayed penalty was called against New Jersey, and Carolina goalie Dan Ellis headed for the bench for an extra attacker. After he left the crease, the Hurricanes accidentally sent the puck the length of the ice back toward their empty net; Ellis tried to race back but was too late. Because Devils goalie Martin Brodeur had been the last Devils player to touch the puck, he was given credit for the goal, and because Ellis was on the ice when the puck went in, the goal went on his record.

1301) Babe Didrikson is the only person named Associated Press athlete of the year in two different sports; she was named for track and field in 1932 and for golf in 1945, 1946, 1947, 1950, and 1954.

1302) President Herbert Hoover was known as "The Great Engineer"; he was a mining engineer who worked around the world and owned a large engineering consulting company.

1303) At 7,000 feet, Santa Fe, New Mexico is the highest elevation state capital.

1304) By area, the Ukraine is the largest country entirely in Europe; it is 223,000 square miles.

1305) London taxi drivers must pass a test called "The Knowledge" which is considered possibly the hardest test in the world. They need to know all of London's 25,000 streets, which way they run, which are one way, and everything on them down to the smallest pub, restaurant and shop. Drivers study for years to pass.

1306) A polar bear's skin is black.

1307) The pizza served in the U.S. each day would cover an area of about 100 acres.

1308) Most birds lack a sense of smell.

1309) Oysters can change their gender based on environmental conditions; they are born male but can change back and forth based on conditions.

1310) The Challenger Deep is the deepest known location in the oceans; it is in the Mariana Trench in the Pacific Ocean and is 36,070 feet deep.

1311) A digamy is a legal second marriage after death or divorce.

1312) Halley's Comet appeared the day Mark Twain was born and the day he died.

1313) In ancient Egypt, men sat to pee and women stood.

1314) Vincent Van Gogh only sold one painting while he was alive.

1315) Andrew Jackson remarried his wife three years after their wedding because her first divorce wasn't finalized.

1316) Octopus blood is blue. It contains a copper rich protein that carries oxygen instead of the iron rich protein in other animals.

1317) At 41 degrees south latitude, Wellington, New Zealand is the world's most southerly national capital.

1318) After dropping out 34 years earlier, Steven Spielberg got his Bachelor of Arts degree from Cal State Long Beach; he submitted *Schindler's List* for credit for his final project in advanced film making.

1319) Neil Armstrong was the first non-military American astronaut in space; he had been a Navy fighter pilot but was a civilian when he joined NASA.

1320) Hilary Clinton was the first U.S. first lady to be elected to public office.

1321) Rats can't vomit which makes them particularly vulnerable to poison.

1322) The Eiffel Tower was originally intended for Barcelona; Spain rejected the project.

1323) Nebraska has the most miles of rivers of any state; it has four major rivers - Platte, Niobrara, Missouri, and Republican.

1324) Astronauts in space are trained to go to the bathroom every two hours because you can't tell if your bladder is full in space.

1325) Millard Fillmore was the last president who wasn't either a Democrat or Republican; he was a member of the Whig party.

1326) A gross is equal to 144 units; a great gross is 1,728 units or 12 gross.

1327) An average adult English speaker has 20,000 words in their vocabulary.

1328) The ancient Romans used human urine to wash clothes.

1329) South Africa has three national capital cities. Pretoria is the administrative capital; Cape Town is the legislative capital, and Bloemfontein is the judicial capital.

1330) The praying mantis is the only insect that can turn its head.

1331) Miami is the only major U.S. city founded by a woman; Julia Tuttle was a businesswoman and the original owner of the land upon which Miami was built.

1332) The Eiffel Tower wasn't intended to be permanent; it was scheduled for demolition in 1909 but was saved to be used as a radio tower.

1333) Based on number of participants, soccer is the most popular sport in the world; badminton is second, and field hockey is third.

1334) There are no landlocked countries in North America.

1335) In Spanish, the word esposas means both wives and handcuffs.

1336) Tomatoes are the most popular crop in U.S. home vegetable gardens.

1337) Camel hair brushes are typically made from squirrel hair.

1338) Before Facebook, Mark Zuckerberg initially created a website to rate the attractiveness of female Harvard students called FaceMash; he received a six-month academic probation for it.

1339) Iceland was the first country to legalize abortion in 1935.

1340) La Rinconada, Peru is the world's highest elevation city; it is a mining town at 16,700 feet in the Andes and has about 30,000 residents.

1341) NFL quarterback Fran Tarkenton's scrambling style was largely responsible for the addition of a line judge to monitor line of scrimmage infractions in 1965.

1342) Barbra Streisand is the only person to win Oscars for Best Actress and Best Song; she won the Best Actress Oscar for *Funny Girl* (1968) and the Best Original Song Oscar for "Evergreen" from *A Star is Born* (1976).

1343) Abraham Lincoln is the only U.S. president ever awarded a patent; it was for a device that helped buoy vessels over shoals.

1344) In 1975, *Jaws* was the first movie to make $100 million at the box office.

1345) A female cat is called a molly; after she becomes a mother, she is called a queen.

1346) The Hundred Years War between England and France lasted 116 years from 1337 to 1453.

1347) The terms uppercase and lowercase regarding letters originated in early print shops. The individual pieces of metal type were kept in boxes called cases; the smaller, more frequently used letters were kept in a lower case that was easier to reach; the less frequently used capital letters were kept in the upper case.

1348) Franklin D. Roosevelt was the first president to use an armored car; the car previously belonged to Al Capone.

1349) Forty percent of schizophrenics are left-handed; only 10% of the total population is left-handed.

1350) The Sun accounts for 99.8% of our solar system's total mass.

1351) The Moon and Sun fit together so perfectly in a solar eclipse because the Sun is about 400 times larger than the Moon, and it is also about 400 times further away from the Earth, so the two appear to be the same size in the sky.

1352) Louis Armstrong is the oldest artist to have a number one hit on Billboard's Hot 100 at age 62 with "Hello Dolly" in 1964.

1353) Satchel Paige was the oldest Major League Baseball rookie at age 42.

1354) Frenchwoman Micheline Ostermeyer won the shot put and discus at the 1948 London Olympics; she also was a professional concert pianist. She had never picked up a discus until a few weeks before winning the Olympic title; she also won bronze in the 80-meter hurdles.

1355) Sunsets on Mars are blue.

1356) In search of perpetual motion, Blaise Pascal invented the roulette wheel in the 17th century.

1357) The sooty shearwater has the world's longest distance migration. It is a common seabird and has been tracked electronically migrating 40,000 miles.

1358) Norway, Austria, and Liechtenstein are the only countries that have won more medals at the Winter Olympics than at the Summer Olympics.

1359) Natural vanilla flavoring comes from orchids.

1360) Tiffany's supplied the Union army with swords and surgical instruments during the Civil War.

1361) In the human body, a limbal dermoid is a cyst in the eye formed in the womb when skin cells get misplaced in the eye; the cyst can grow hair, cartilage, sweat glands, and even teeth like skin can.

1362) James Madison was the lightest president at 100 pounds.

1363) Based on land area, the city of Hulunbuir in China is the largest city in the world; it is 102,000 square miles or about the size of Colorado.

1364) Europe is the only continent without a significant desert.

1365) *The Passion of the Christ* (2004) is the highest grossing foreign language or subtitled film ever in the U.S.

1366) The Congo is the only river that crosses the equator in both a northerly and southerly direction.

1367) Liechtenstein is the only country to have won medals in the Winter Olympics but never in the Summer Olympics.

1368) The British navy plays Britney Spears music to help scare off Somali pirates.

1369) The earliest known reference to a vending machine is in 1st century Egypt. It dispensed holy water; when a coin was deposited, it fell on a pan attached to a lever. The lever opened a valve which let some water flow out. The pan continued to tilt with the weight of the coin until it fell off at which point a counterweight snapped the lever up and turned off the valve.

1370) A pangram is a sentence or verse that contains all letters in the alphabet at least once such as "The quick brown fox jumps over a lazy dog."

1371) In music, a semihemidemisemiquaver is a 1/128th note.

1372) Search engines can access about 0.03% of the internet. About 99.96% of the internet is the deep web which is anything that is password protected, requires filling out a form, etc. such as email, social media profiles, databases, etc. The tiny remaining portion is the dark web which is a subset of the deep web and is encrypted for illegal or secretive purposes.

1373) Chuck Berry's only number one hit was "My Ding-a-ling."

1374) Calvin Coolidge had a pet raccoon while in the White House; the raccoon was a gift and was supposed to be served for Thanksgiving dinner. Coolidge made it a pet and even walked it on a leash on the White House grounds.

1375) Bangkok, Thailand is the most visited city in the world; London is second.

1376) J.R.R. Tolkien coined the word tween in *The Hobbit*; he used it to describe Hobbits in their reckless age period.

1377) Bob Richards was the first athlete to appear on the front of the Wheaties box; he appeared in 1958 after being the 1952 and 1956 Olympic pole vault gold medalist.

1378) *Seven Samurai* (1954) is often credited as the first modern action film using elements such as slow motion for dramatic effect.

1379) In 1892, Juan Vucetich was the first person to solve a crime using fingerprints.

1380) Andrew Jackson is the only president to be held as a prisoner of war; he joined the Revolutionary War at age 13 and was captured by the British.

1381) *Mary Poppins* in 1964 was the only film personally produced by Walt Disney to be nominated for the Best Picture Oscar.

1382) Iceland has the oldest parliament in the world; it has existed since 930 AD.

1383) At the ancient Olympic games, they used tethered doves as archery targets.

1384) Alaska is the only state name that can be typed on one row of a standard keyboard.

1385) Eighty percent of all the paragraphs written in English contain the word the.

1386) Ancient Egyptians shaved off their own eyebrows to mourn the deaths of their cats.

1387) The giant armadillo has the most teeth (up to 100) of any land animal.

1388) Q-tips were originally called Baby Gays. They were originally for babies' eyes, ears, nostrils, and gums; the Q stands for quality.

1389) The foam on beer is called barm.

1390) Benjamin Franklin first suggested the idea of daylight saving time in an essay he wrote in 1784.

1391) Bananas are the most frequently sold item at Walmart.

1392) A giraffe has the highest blood pressure of any animal; it is about 300 over 200.

1393) The eruption of Krakatoa in 1883 is the loudest sound in recorded history; it ruptured people's eardrums 40 miles away and was clearly heard 3,000 miles away.

1394) The male honeybee's testicles explode on mating, and then he dies.

1395) The U.S. Congress allowed 15 years for voluntary conversion to the metric system in legislation passed in 1975.

1396) Table tennis balls were originally made from cork from wine bottles.

1397) Giraffes need the least sleep of any mammal; they only sleep 30 minutes a day on average just a few minutes at a time.

1398) W is the shortest three syllable word in English. The letters of the alphabet are generally also considered words since they are nouns referring to the letter.

1399) Amen is in 1,200 different languages without change.

1400) Sulfur gives onions their distinctive smell; when cut or crushed, a chemical reaction changes an amino acid into a sulfur compound.

1401) The Netherlands has on average the tallest people in the world with an average of 5'11 1/2" for men and 5'6 1/2" for women.

1402) The Red Sea is the world's warmest sea.

1403) Mercury was used in the production of felt which led to the expression "mad as a hatter" due to mercury poisoning.

1404) Eleven of the twelve men who walked on the Moon were Boy Scouts.

1405) At 19,341 feet, Mount Kilimanjaro is the world's highest mountain that isn't part of a range.

1406) Abraham Lincoln was the tallest U.S. president at 6'4".

1407) Fred Perry is the only person to be number one in the world in both table tennis and tennis. He won the 1929 world championship in table tennis and was the first player in tennis to win a career grand slam including three straight Wimbledon titles from 1934-1936.

1408) The stapes in the middle ear is the smallest bone in the human body.

1409) Pandiculating is stretching and stiffening your trunk and extremities as when fatigued, drowsy, or waking - like a cat.

1410) Bagpipes were invented in the Middle East.

1411) With 22 competitive and 4 honorary awards, Walt Disney won more Oscars than any other individual.

1412) At 5,000 years old, the bristlecone pine species is the oldest living individual tree.

1413) There are about 10 times more bacterial cells in the human body than there are body cells.

1414) The probability that any single glass of water contains at least one molecule of water drunk by Cleopatra is almost 100%. There are about 1,000 times as many molecules of water in a glass as there are glasses of water in the Earth's water supply. If water molecules spread through the entire water supply, any given glass of water should contain 1,000 molecules of water from any other given glass.

1415) Spain kept the discovery of chocolate a national secret for nearly a century.

1416) Gerald Ford is the only Eagle Scout to become president.

1417) The closest living relative to the Tyrannosaurus Rex is the chicken.

1418) *The French Connection* (1971) was the first R-rated movie to win the Best Picture Oscar.

1419) George Solti has won the most Grammy Awards with 31.

1420) The Wall Street area in New York City is named after a barrier built by the Dutch in the 17th century to protect against Indian attacks.

1421) Based on global following, soccer is the most popular sport in the world; cricket is second; field hockey is third.

1422) The *Mona Lisa* is painted on wood, a thin poplar panel.

1423) About 40% of the world's cultures engage in romantic kissing.

1424) *Ben-Hur: A Tale of the Christ* was the first fictional novel blessed by the pope.

1425) Peter Sellers was the first man to appear on the cover of *Playboy*.

1426) The cast of *Glee* has the most Billboard Hot 100 entries of all time with 207.

1427) The first Olympics televised in the U.S. were the Squaw Valley, California 1960 Winter Olympics.

1428) Rodents have more species than any other mammal.

1429) Adjusted for inflation, *Butch Cassidy and the Sundance Kid* (1969) is the highest grossing western of all time in the U.S.

1430) A moth grub moving inside the bean causes a jumping bean to jump.

1431) Before he assumed office, Pope Pius II wrote one of the most popular books of the 15th century; it was an erotic novel, the tale of two lovers.

1432) The loudest instrument in a standard orchestra is the trombone which peaks at about 115 decibels.

1433) Pepsi was the first U.S. consumer product sold in the former Soviet Union.

1434) The United States has more tornadoes than any other country.

1435) A group of elk is called a gang.

1436) The Tour de France bicycle race has the most in person spectators of any single sporting event in the world. It attracts 12 to 15 million spectators.

1437) Political cartoonist Thomas Nast popularized the use of the elephant and donkey as symbols of the two main U.S. political parties; he also created the image of the modern Santa Claus.

1438) Theodore Roosevelt was the first American to win a Nobel Prize of any kind. He won the 1906 Peace Prize; the Nobel Prizes started in 1901.

1439) Apples, peaches, and raspberries belong to the rose plant family.

1440) Bird's nest soup is made from the nests of swifts; the nest is saliva that has dried and hardened.

1441) Australia is the only continent without glaciers.

1442) Austin, Texas is the largest population city in the U.S. that doesn't have an MLB, NFL, NBA, or NHL team; it is the 11th largest city in U.S.

1443) The hard piece at the end of a shoelace is called an aglet.

1444) Mozart and Beethoven composed music for the glass armonica instrument which was invented by Benjamin Franklin. It replicated the sound a wet finger makes when rubbed along the rim of a glass; it became very popular, and quite a few composers wrote pieces for it.

1445) Of the seven wonders of the ancient world, only the Great Pyramid of Giza still exists. The Lighthouse at Alexandria was the last wonder to disappear; it was toppled by earthquakes in the early 14th century, and its ruined stones were carried off by the late 15th century.

1446) Beijing will be the first city to host both the summer and winter Olympics. It hosted the 2008 summer games and will host the 2022 winter games.

1447) The Nile crocodile has the greatest bite force of any animal; it can bite down with 5,000 psi.

1448) A cluster of 10-20 bananas is called a hand.

1449) U.S. President Barack Obama's mother had the first name Stanley.

1450) The monkeys Mizaru, Kikazaru, and Iwazaru are better known as see no evil, hear no evil, and speak no evil.

1451) Janis Joplin, Jimi Hendrix, and Kurt Cobain all died at age 27.

1452) When you die, hearing is the last sense to go.

1453) The Afghan War is the longest war in U.S. history.

1454) *The Shape of Water* in 2017 was the first science fiction film to win the Best Picture Oscar?

1455) The sperm whale has the largest brain of any animal. A sperm whale's brain is about 17 pounds compared to 3 pounds for a human.

1456) At age 32, Sally Ride is the youngest American astronaut in space.

1457) *SportsCenter* on ESPN has aired the most episodes ever for any U.S. television show. It has broadcast over 50,000 unique episodes since 1979.

1458) Beards were taxed in Elizabethan times.

1459) The longest time period any sports trophy has been successfully defended is 132 years. The America's Cup for sailing was held by the United States from its start in 1851 until Australia won in 1983.

1460) Australia is the only continent without an active volcano.

1461) A normal house cat has 18 claws; there are five on each front paw and four on each back paw.

1462) The world's oldest snack food is the pretzel dating back to the 6th century.

1463) The Moon is moving away from the Earth by about 1.5 inches per year.

1464) Chris Elliot was the first *Saturday Night Live* cast member to also have their child become a cast member.

1465) Uruguay is the first country in the world to fully legalize marijuana; it took full effect in 2017.

1466) Four U.S. presidents have won the Nobel Peace Prize - Theodore Roosevelt, Woodrow Wilson, Jimmy Carter, Barack Obama.

1467) Albert Einstein called income taxes "the hardest thing in the world to understand."

1468) Santa Fe, New Mexico is the only two-word state capital in a two-word state.

1469) The U.S. has the most dogs of any country in the world; Brazil has the second most.

1470) During the Boer War from 1900-1902, Great Britain originated the concept of the concentration camp.

1471) Rio de Janeiro, Brazil was the only European capital outside of Europe; it was capital of Portugal from 1808 to 1822. Napoleon was invading Portugal at the time, so the Portuguese royal family moved to Rio, and it became the capital.

1472) At its closest point, the distance between the U.S. and Russia is 2.4 miles.

1473) Human babies have 300 bones; some fuse together to form the 206 bones in adults.

1474) By 70 years of age, the average person will have shed 105 pounds of skin.

1475) For Thomas Edison's death in 1931, all non-essential lights in the U.S. were turned off for one minute in his honor.

1476) You would swim the same speed through syrup as you do through water; the additional drag is canceled out by the additional force generated from each stroke.

1477) Thirty-five percent of the world's population drives on the left side.

1478) Divorce is still illegal in the Philippines and Vatican City.

1479) Of the 48 contiguous states, Austin, Texas is the most southern state capital.

1480) Famed U.S. WWII General George S. Patton placed fifth in the pentathlon at the 1912 Olympics.

1481) In ancient Greece, throwing an apple at someone was a declaration of love.

1482) Delaware has the lowest average elevation of any state at just 60 feet.

1483) During WWII when Hitler visited Paris, the French cut the Eiffel Tower lift cables, so Hitler would have to climb the steps if he wanted to go to the top.

1484) Frank Lloyd Wright's son John invented Lincoln Logs after watching workers move timber.

1485) Phidipedes ran the first marathon upon which all others are based. He ran 140 miles round trip from Athens to Sparta over mountain terrain to ask for military aid, marched 26 miles from Athens to Marathon, fought all morning, and then ran 26 miles to Athens with the victory news and died of exhaustion.

1486) Thomas Edison is credited with suggesting the word hello be used when answering a telephone; Alexander Graham Bell thought ahoy was better.

1487) The New Testament was originally written in Greek.

1488) New Zealand bans television advertising on Christmas, Easter, and Good Friday.

1489) Great Britain is the only country to win a gold medal at every Summer Olympics. Due to boycotts, only Great Britain, France,

Australia, Greece, and Switzerland have participated in every Summer Olympics.

1490) There are 45 miles of nerves in the human body.

1491) Banana cream was the original flavor of the Twinkie filling.

1492) Delaware has the fewest counties of any state with three.

1493) There are 293 possible ways to make change for a dollar.

1494) Venus has a longer day than its year. It takes 243 days for one rotation (1 day) and 225 days for one orbit around the Sun (1 year).

1495) The S in Harry S. Truman's name didn't stand for anything; it was in honor of both his grandfathers but didn't stand for a middle name.

1496) Chang is the most common surname in the world.

1497) Only the nine banded armadillo and humans are known to be infected with leprosy.

1498) The company Google was originally called Backrub.

1499) The British pound is the world's oldest currency still in use; it is 1,200 years old.

1500) Many U.S. police departments adopted navy blue uniforms because they were surplus army uniforms from the Civil War.

Made in the USA
Columbia, SC
01 June 2019